TURNING POINT IN TIMBER CONSTRUCTION

T0326682

TURNING POINT IN TIMBER CONSTRUCTION

A New Economy

Ulrich Dangel

Birkhäuser
Basel

Preface

Our society is currently faced with two major challenges: man-made climate change and the need to provide housing for an ever-increasing world population. Since the Industrial Revolution, we have relied on steel and concrete as the major building materials for the construction of our cities. Their refinement and processing requires large amounts of energy, mostly generated by the burning of fossil fuels. As a result, carbon stored over millions of years has been released into the Earth's atmosphere within the relatively short period of about one hundred and fifty years in the form of carbon dioxide, contributing significantly to the climate shift we are experiencing today. The manufacture of cement (the key ingredient of concrete), in particular, produces one ton of carbon dioxide for every ton of cement. It constitutes one of the most polluting processes in the construction industry. In order to provide sufficient housing for future generations while lessening the impact on our environment, we must rethink the way we will build in the future.

Wood is a truly renewable building material that is unlimited in supply if its growth and harvest are sustainably managed. Trees store carbon through photosynthesis as they grow, simultaneously releasing oxygen. When wood decays or burns, it only releases as much carbon dioxide into the atmosphere as has been bound during its growth, therefore completing a carbon-neutral life cycle. Recent technological advancements in engineering allow the use of timber for the construction of multi-story structures, turning our buildings and cities into carbon sinks rather than sources of CO_2 emissions. This book presents compelling arguments for the increased use of wood as an alternative to fossil fuel-based building materials, with the goal of demonstrating that an integrated approach can have the potential for positive impact on the environment, local economies, and the building culture at large.

Ulrich Dangel
AIA, NCARB, ARB, Dipl.-Ing. Architekt
Austin, Texas, Spring 2016

CONTENTS

Foreword

We are living at a decisive turning point in history. Changes in our lifestyle are necessary if we are to provide our descendants with a livable future. The transition from the fossil to the biogenic fuel age is underway and in many areas of daily life, efforts and developments toward sustainable strategies are visible. These issues are still relatively new and have only been a focus of genuine concern for recent generations. When I studied architecture forty years ago, there was no mention of resource-efficient construction. As the son of a carpenter, I was also surprised by the lack of motivation and the antiquated approach that characterized the way building with timber was conveyed to us as prospective architects. Modernism, with its preferred materials of steel and concrete, was still prevalent, which resulted in timber construction simply being forgotten.

However, this is currently changing worldwide. After twenty years of research and development into reducing the operational energy of buildings, along with the introduction of renewable energy sources, the question of how to deal with an increasing scarcity of resources has emerged. The call for renewable raw materials is particularly clear in the construction sector, and as a result, due to its availability and unique properties, wood has come to be seen as a material that holds great promise for the future of building. While just a few years ago multi-story construction in wood was considered inconceivable, we have now reached heights of eighteen stories today, and the building volumes of completed projects are steadily increasing as well. This is accompanied by evidence that wood is returning to the urban realm, a trend that will continue if appropriate measures are adopted. Above all, this includes the comprehensive education of all relevant professions. Experience has clearly shown that a high level of knowledge is a prerequisite for the successful implementation of a new timber construction strategy. This applies to the entire chain, ranging from the forestry sector, to sawmill and wood processing industries, to carpentry businesses – in particular their employees – to the planning and design professions, and not least, the approval authorities. Significant demands are therefore placed on a number of educational institutions, particularly those offering professional and specialist training in the specific building trades, as well as the academic education for engineers and architects. In parallel, there is the need to increase subject-specific publications in order to provide all concerned with current and in-depth information on state of the art technical developments, while also intensifying efforts to establish standards for assembly, detailing, and building physics to simplify building with timber. This focused development has been necessary in the case of all modern building methods, and timber construction will similarly require sufficient time and coordinated resources in order to achieve these educational and standardization goals. In my opinion, the current development of timber construction is bound to accelerate given the clear political and social will to build more sustainably.

This book by Ulrich Dangel presents a comprehensive narrative of timber construction in an interesting and accessible manner. By tracing all steps from the forest to the finished building, it provides a long-overdue and important incentive for the reintroduction of an old building tradition under new premises. The fundamental realization that it is both sensible and urgent to consider renewable resources as the modern materials of the future can serve as motivation to follow this path forward. This book represents an important contribution to the development of such an understanding.

Hermann Kaufmann
Univ.-Prof. DI

The World's Forests

Today, forests cover about 4 billion hectares globally, which represents approximately 30 percent of the Earth's total land area.[1] Forest vegetation is distributed in large bands around the planet, and their composition and characteristics are affected by the latitude and the corresponding climate zone. Satellite images reveal three distinct patterns: The boreal forest close to the North Pole extends across large parts of Alaska, Canada, Scandinavia, and Russia. Situated further away from the pole, the temperate forest of the northern hemisphere is widely distributed across North America, Europe, and Asia. Due to the higher ratio of sea to land in the other hemisphere, its southern counterpart only covers relatively small coastal areas of South America, southern Africa, Australia, and New Zealand. Third, the band of subtropical and tropical forests reaches from Central and South America across Africa to the Indian subcontinent and Southeast Asia.[2]

Forests are the predominant and biologically most diverse ecosystems on land, and they provide habitat for more than 80 percent of the terrestrial species of animals, plants, and insects.[3] The number of people that benefit from the use of forest products to satisfy their basic needs for food, energy, and shelter is in the billions.[4] Forests provide mankind not only with wood, which is one of its most sustainable resources, but also with a number of important non-timber forest products (NTFP) including rubber, cork, fruit, and ingredients for pharmaceuticals.[5] Wood fuel such as firewood and charcoal is often the only energy source in the rural areas of less developed countries, and it is estimated that about 2.4 billion people worldwide cook with it. In the form of chips and pellets, wood is also being used increasingly for domestic heating in developed countries, with the goal of reducing dependence on fossil fuels.[6] Forests play a critical role in the hydrological cycle, since they regulate surface and groundwater flows and contribute to maintaining high water quality through natural filtration. They aid in the prevention of soil erosion, landslides, floods, and droughts as well as helping to reduce the risk of desertification and salinization. Forested watersheds feed the rivers and are essential to supplying a large portion of the world's fresh water for domestic, agricultural, and industrial use.[7] By modulating air temperature and moisture levels, forests can create favorable microclimates conducive to growing cash crops in certain regions.[8]

The oxygen in the air that all living things breathe is the result of photosynthesis: a natural process through which trees and plants use energy from the sun to create the food they need to live and grow. Water and minerals from the soil are transported from the roots to a tree's needles or leaves, which simultaneously collect carbon dioxide from the atmosphere. Chlorophyll, a biomolecule contained in specialized cells called chloroplasts, uses sunlight energy to convert the carbon dioxide (CO_2) and water into oxygen (O_2) and carbohydrates such as glucose – a vital nutrient that the tree needs for growth. The tree releases the resulting oxygen into the atmosphere, thereby supporting all human and animal life.[9] By removing CO_2 from the atmosphere, forests and photosynthesis also play a crucial role in reducing the impact of CO_2 emissions on the environment.

Forests provide numerous benefits to the health of the planet and the well-being of its inhabitants, and preserving these vitally important ecosystems against competing human interests is one of the world's greatest challenges.

1 *Global Forest Resources Assessment 2015.* Food and Agriculture Organization of the United Nations, 2015. 3.   2 Pan, Yude. "The Structure, Distribution, and Biomass of the World's Forests." *Annual Review of Ecology, Evolution, and Systematics* Vol. 44 (2013). 595.   3 *Vital Forest Graphics.* United Nations Environment Programme, Food and Agriculture Organization of the United Nations, United Nations Forum on Forests, 2009. 38.   4 *State of the World's Forests 2014.* Rome: Food and Agriculture Organization of the United Nations, 2014. xiii.   5 Wegener, Gerd. "Forests and their Significance." *Building with Timber: Paths into the Future.* Eds. Hermann Kaufmann and Winfried Nerdinger. Munich: Prestel, 2011. 10.   6 *State of the World's Forests 2014.* xiii.   7 *Forests and Water: International Momentum and Action.* Rome: Food and Agriculture Organization of the United Nations, 2013. 1–2.   8 *Vital Forest Graphics.* 33.   9 *Fact Sheet: Photosynthesis.* Portland: Oregon Forest Resources Institute.

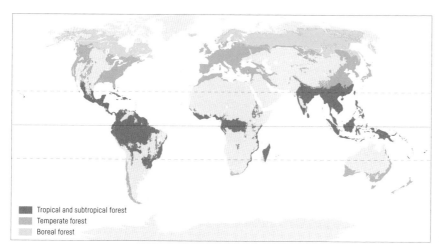

Tropical and subtropical forest
Temperate forest
Boreal forest

1

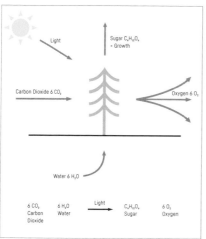

Light

Sugar C₆H₁₂O₆
= Growth

Carbon Dioxide 6 CO₂

Oxygen 6 O₂

Water 6 H₂O

| 6 CO₂ Carbon Dioxide | 6 H₂O Water | Light | C₆H₁₂O₆ Sugar | 6 O₂ Oxygen |

2

3

1 Forests of the world   **2** Photosynthesis   **3** Boreal
forest in Northern Finland   **4** Tropical rainforest
in Thailand   **5** Temperate forest in the United States

Deforestation

Deforestation is defined as the permanent conversion of forest land to non-forest land and it happens for many different reasons in all regions of the world. Population increase and the resulting demand for more land can be identified as significant underlying causes of deforestation.[1] Trees are cut down to be used or sold as fuel or timber, but some of the most serious deforestation occurs when land is cleared for agricultural use, in particular for the cultivation of highly profitable commodity crops such as palm oil, soybeans, sugar cane, and rice. Forests are also frequently cleared for livestock pasture to enable meat production.[2] Contrary to popular belief, the harvesting of tropical timber is rarely the main cause of deforestation. The establishment of logging roads, however, tends to provide easy access to previously undisturbed areas, thus facilitating the clearance of these forests and their conversion to other land uses.[3]

Over the last twenty-five years, the world has seen a reduction of its forest area from 4.1 billion hectares to just under 4 billion hectares, which is equivalent to a decrease of 3.1 percent.[4] Tracking global forest gains and losses is a complex undertaking that is very difficult to monitor, even with high-resolution satellite imagery.[5] Throughout history, deforestation has been more widespread in temperate regions than in subtropical and tropical regions. As a result, Europe is the continent with the smallest portion of its original forests remaining today.[6] Recently however, the rate at which forest has been converted to other land has been greatest in the tropics, which have recorded continuous losses since 1990.[7] As a result of globalization, many tropical developing countries are responding to market demands and are capitalizing on new export opportunities. This accelerates the rate at which deforestation takes place, often through slash-and-burn practices, which involve cutting and burning native forest so as to replace it with agricultural crops and animal pasture. The countries reporting the greatest annual reductions in forest area include Brazil, the world's second biggest soybean and beef producer, and Indonesia, a major supplier of palm oil.[8] Myanmar, Nigeria, and Tanzania round out the list of the top five countries experiencing the highest net losses. In contrast, net forest area has increased in the temperate countries, including Australia, Chile, and the United States, while China in particular is leading the way with large-scale afforestation programs.[9] The forest land gain in the developed world can be traced back to fundamental changes in farming practices that occurred in the 1940s and 1950s, when agriculture moved away from animal power to tractors and mechanical equipment. Increased productivity, substantial gains in crop yields, and the dwindling need for pasture land allowed more farmland to become forested again, a trend that continues today.[10] In the boreal and subtropical climate zones, relatively little change in forest area has been observed.[11]

Besides fossil fuel combustion, deforestation is considered to be the second largest contributing factor in carbon dioxide emissions to the atmosphere. Deforestation and forest degradation are responsible for 12 percent of human-generated greenhouse gases, which are released by clearance work, the burning of forest biomass, and the decomposition of plant material and soil carbon.[12] Not only does the removal of trees without sufficient reforestation adversely affect the forest's carbon storage and sequestration potential, it also involves the loss of all resources – timber and non-wood forest products – as well as negative impacts on water, soil, and biodiversity.[13] One effort to assign a financial value to the carbon stored in forests is the United Nation's Reducing Emissions from Deforestation and Forest Degradation (REDD) program, which offers incentives and strategic approaches for developing countries to conserve forested land and manage it sustainably.[14] This initiative is considered by many to be a promising solution in combating global climate change.[15] The fate of the world's forests will depend on good governance, sound land and resource rights, and the development of more sustainable and more efficient strategies for growing food and producing commodities.[16]

1 *Vital Forest Graphics.* United Nations Environment Programme, Food and Agriculture Organization of the United Nations, United Nations Forum on Forests, 2009. 12. **2** *Vital Forest Graphics.* 20–23. **3** *Vital Forest Graphics.* 11–12. **4** *Global Forest Resources Assessment 2015.* Food and Agriculture Organization of the United Nations, 2015. 14. **5** *Global Forest Resources Assessment 2015.* 3. **6** *Vital Forest Graphics.* 11. **7** *Global Forest Resources Assessment 2015.* 14. **8** *Vital Forest Graphics.* 20–23. **9** *Global Forest Resources Assessment 2015.* 15. **10** Fernholz, Kathryn. "Understanding Your Environment: Forest, Trees, and Responsible Wood Products." Austin, Texas. 22 Jan. 2014. Lecture. **11** *Global Forest Resources Assessment 2015.* 14. **12** Van der Werf, Guido R. "CO$_2$ Emissions from Forest Loss." *Nature Geoscience* Vol. 2. November (2009): 737. **13** *Vital Forest Graphics.* 12. **14** "United Nations Environment Programme." *REDD+.* Web. 14 Sept. 2015. **15** *Vital Forest Graphics.* 12. **16** Nigel Sizer. "Tree Cover Loss Spikes in Russia and Canada, Remains High Globally." World Resources Institute, 02 Apr. 2015. Web. 14 Sept. 2015.

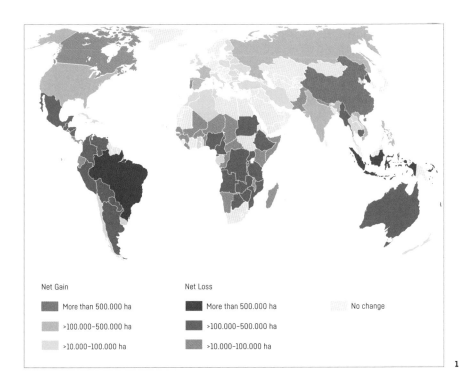

Net Gain

More than 500.000 ha

>100.000–500.000 ha

>10.000–100.000 ha

Net Loss

More than 500.000 ha

>100.000–500.000 ha

>10.000–100.000 ha

No change

1

2

3

4

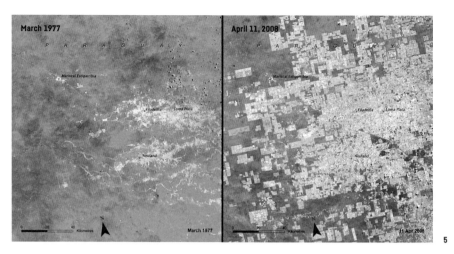

March 1977

April 11, 2008

March 1977

11 Apr 2008

5

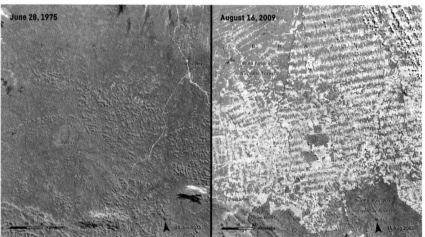

June 28, 1975

August 16, 2009

28 Jun 1975

16 Aug 2009

6

1 Annual net forest gain and loss by country (1990–2015)   **2** Slash-and-burn farming in Rondônia, western Brazil   **3** Several fires burning in Pará, Brazil to clear patches of forest for agriculture. Photographed from the International Space Station (ISS).
4 Deforestation   **5** Change in land use due to livestock production and agriculture, Gran Chaco, Paraguay.
6 Land use change in Rondônia, which has the highest deforestation rate in the Brazilian Amazon.

Climate Change

Throughout history, the climate of the Earth has fluctuated. Glacial advance and re-
treat have alternated in cycles, with the last ice age ending abruptly about seven
thousand years ago and thus facilitating the development of human civilization.
Most of the associated temperature variations can be attributed to changes in the
planet's orbit around the sun and the amount of solar radiation it received during
a particular period.[1] The warming trends currently being experienced are, however, unprecedented throughout history; moreover they have been documented by measurements of rising surface air and subsurface ocean temperatures.[2]
The period from 1983 to 2012 was most likely the warmest thirty-year period of
the last fourteen hundred years in the northern hemisphere.[3] Increasing global
temperatures have been accompanied by changes in the weather and climates:
Sea levels are rising; oceans are warming and becoming more acidic; glaciers
are retreating; ice sheets and sea ice are declining, and snow cover is decreasing.[4] Many locations around the world are witnessing a growing frequency of
extreme events, including heavy rainfall, floods, droughts, and landslides.[5]

There is a strong consensus in the scientific community that global climate change
is a direct result of human activity.[6] Greenhouse gases in the atmosphere absorb and reradiate solar energy that would otherwise be reflected back into
space. Without them, the Earth would have extreme temperature fluctuations,
which would make it impossible to sustain life as it currently exists. However,
anthropogenic emissions of carbon dioxide, methane, nitrous oxide, and chloro-
fluorocarbons are altering the natural greenhouse effect and are leading to atmospheric concentrations that are unprecedented.[7] Through the combustion of
fossil fuels, for instance, carbon dioxide levels have increased from 280 ppm in
1750 to over 400 ppm today, which is higher than any previous levels that have
been recorded for the last 420,000 years.[8] This increase in greenhouse gases is
thought to be responsible for the warming observed since the mid-20th century.[9] Continued emissions into the atmosphere will cause further temperature
rises and long-lasting changes to the weather and climates, increasing the likelihood of severe and irreversible consequences for people and the planet.[10]

Presently, the only climate treaty with broad legitimacy resides within the *United
Nations Framework Convention on Climate Change* (UNFCC), whereby the international community has agreed to combat climate change by limiting the increase
of global average temperature to 2°C above pre-industrial times.[11] Mitigation
strategies to limit warming will require substantial reductions of emissions over
the next few decades, as well as near zero emissions of CO_2 and other long-lived
greenhouse gases by the end of the 21st century.[12] Unsustainable consumption
and manufacturing with a heavy reliance on fossil fuels are at the root of the
problem, so transitioning toward resilient, low-carbon societies and economies
will be vital in attempting to mitigate the adverse impacts of climate change.

1 "Climate Change Evidence: How Do We Know?" *Climate Change: Vital Signs of the Planet.* NASA. Web. 15 Sept. 2015.   **2** *Joint Science Academies' Statement: Global Response to Climate Change.* Washington, DC: National Academies of Sciences, Engineering, Medicine, 2005.   **3** Core Writing Team, Rajendra K. Pachauri, and Leo Meyer, eds. *Climate Change 2014: Synthesis Report. Contribution of Working Groups I, II and III to the Fifth Assessment Report of the Intergovernmental Panel on Climate Change.* Geneva: IPCC, 2015. 2.   **4** "Climate Change Evidence: How Do We Know?" 15 Sept. 2015.   **5** "Climate Change: Basic Information." *EPA. Environmental Protection Agency.* Web. 15 Sept. 2015.   **6** *A Summary of Current Climate Change Findings and Figures.* Geneva: World Meteorological Organization, 2013. 1.   **7** Core Writing Team, Rajendra K. Pachauri, and Leo Meyer, eds. 4.   **8** *Joint Science Academies' Statement: Global Response to Climate Change.* 2005.   **9** Core Writing Team, Rajendra K. Pachauri, and Leo Meyer, eds. 4.   **10** Core Writing Team, Rajendra K. Pachauri, and Leo Meyer, eds. 56.   **11** European Environment Agency. *EEA SIGNALS 2015: Living in a Changing Climate.* Luxembourg: Publications Office of the European Union, 2015. 6.   **12** Core Writing Team, Rajendra K. Pachauri, and Leo Meyer, eds. 56.

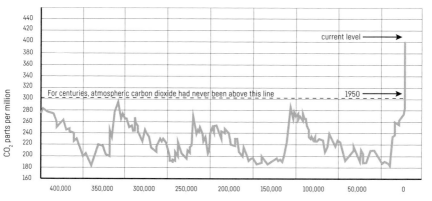

Jul. 28, 1986

Jul. 2, 2014

4

1941

2004

5

2000

2007

2015

6

1 Atmospheric carbon dioxide levels   **2** Global land-
ocean temperature index (5-year mean)   **3** Greenhouse
effect   **4** Alaska's Columbia Glacier began retreating
rapidly in the 1980s.   **5** Muir Glacier melt, Alaska
6 Aral Sea shrinkage, central Asia

The Carbon Cycle and Forests

Carbon is the fourth most abundant element in the universe and it forms the basis of all known life. It is found in every living organism and many non-living substances, including human beings, plants, soils, and the air. Carbon is stored in carbon "pools" or "reservoirs," which include the oceans, the land and its vegetation, and the atmosphere. Each carbon reservoir can act as a source by emitting carbon, or serve as a sink by absorbing carbon. The dynamic exchange or "flux" of carbon between pools is described as the carbon cycle. It plays a critical role in regulating the Earth's climate, since maintaining the right concentration of carbon dioxide in the atmosphere helps to ensure stable average temperatures on a global scale.[1] In the absence of human intervention, the natural two-way flow of biogenic carbon between the atmosphere and living organisms in the oceans and on land remained relatively balanced. Through photosynthesis, plants absorb and store carbon, which is released again once the plants die. Over millions of years, however, organic matter buried deep in ocean sediments (and thus protected from decay) has been transformed into hydrocarbons, forming large deposits of coal, oil, and natural gas. The combustion of these fossil fuels, along with the conversion of limestone to lime in the process of cement production, have liberated large quantities of carbon from ancient reserves over a relatively short timespan. This one-way flow of fossil carbon, emitted in the form of CO_2, has disrupted the balance of the natural carbon cycle, effectively increasing the amount of greenhouse gases in the atmosphere.[2]

During photosynthesis, trees convert absorbed carbon dioxide into carbon-based compounds that are essential for the growth of new cells. Consequently, about one-half of the dry mass of wood consists of carbon.[3] Besides the tree trunk, carbon is also stored in the branches, bark, roots, and leaves; this means that it is also found in the forest litter and soils. As trees mature, they compete for water, sunlight, and nutrients, which causes some of them to die while others prosper. With increasing age, their growth and, as a result, their carbon capture rate are reduced substantially. Although older forests are able to store more carbon than younger forest stands, they absorb carbon at an ever slower pace.[4] The net carbon storage capacity of an aging forest can even diminish due to greater natural mortality; this stage generally begins once the trees reach an average age of one hundred to one hundred and fifty years. As the number of trees and their age and diameter increase, natural disturbances can also cause severe impacts on affected forest stands. Wildfires, storms, insect infestation, and disease can cause significant tree loss. The death of trees and the decay of their biomass lead to major carbon emissions, which can potentially transform a forest from a carbon sink into a carbon source.[5]

Forests contain 80 percent of the Earth's terrestrial carbon. While they make up a relatively small carbon pool compared with the oceans, their carbon storage potential can readily be influenced through land use policies and sustainable management strategies.[6] There is no doubt that harvesting trees reduces the amount of carbon stored in a forest. However, if a forest is managed responsibly, new tree growth exceeds the number of trees removed, which ensures that carbon stocks remain constant or even increase over time. In contrast to unmanaged forests, trees are harvested before they begin to die, rot, and release CO_2. Sustainable forest management also prevents overcrowding by carrying out selective thinning, which provides the remaining trees with ample room to grow and flourish, greatly reducing the risk of natural disasters such as wildfire or disease outbreaks.[7] Unmanaged forests, on the other hand, can theoretically capture substantial quantities of carbon, but they have a much greater likelihood of carbon loss due to natural disturbances than do managed forests with lower carbon storage capacity and less or no dead and dying fuel wood.[8] Managed forests therefore have a greater long-term potential for reducing CO_2 emissions, even though large amounts of wood are removed from them annually. While the carbon content of the temperate and boreal forests of the world has remained more or less steady over the last one hundred and fifty years as a result of active management, significant carbon losses are occurring in the subtropical and tropical regions, due to deforestation.[9]

1 Lippke, Bruce, Elaine Oneil, Rob Harrison, Kenneth Skog, Leif Gustavsson, and Roger Sathre. "Life Cycle Impacts of Forest Management and Wood Utilization on Carbon Mitigation: Knowns and Unknowns." *Carbon Management* 2.3 (2011). 304. 2 Bowyer, Jim, Steve Bratkovich, Matt Frank, Jeff Howe, Sarah Stai, and Kathryn Fernholz. *Carbon 101: Understanding the Carbon Cycle and the Forest Carbon Debate*. Minneapolis: Dovetail Partners, 2012. 3–4. 3 *Carbon in Wood Products – The Basics*. Minneapolis: Dovetail Partners, 2013. 1. 4 Bowyer, Jim, Steve Bratkovich, Matt Frank, Jeff Howe, Sarah Stai, and Kathryn Fernholz. 4, 7. 5 Bowyer, Jim, Steve Bratkovich, Matt Frank, Kathryn Fernholz, Jeff Howe, and Sarah Stai. *Managing Forests for Carbon Mitigation*. Minneapolis: Dovetail Partners, 2011. 3–4. 6 Wegener, Gerd, and Bernhard Zimmer. "Wald und Holz als Kohlenstoffspeicher und Energieträger – Chancen und Wege für die Forst- und Holzwirtschaft." *Weltforstwirtschaft nach Kyoto. Wald und Holz als Kohlenstoffspeicher und regenerativer Energieträger*. Eds. Andreas Schulte, Klaus Böswald, and Rainer Joosten. Aachen: Shaker Verlag GmbH, 2001. 114. 7 Bowyer, Jim, Steve Bratkovich, Matt Frank, Kathryn Fernholz, Jeff Howe, and Sarah Stai. 5–6. 8 Lippke, Bruce, Elaine Oneil, Rob Harrison, Kenneth Skog, Leif Gustavsson, and Roger Sathre. 309. 9 Wegener, Gerd, and Bernhard Zimmer. 115.

2

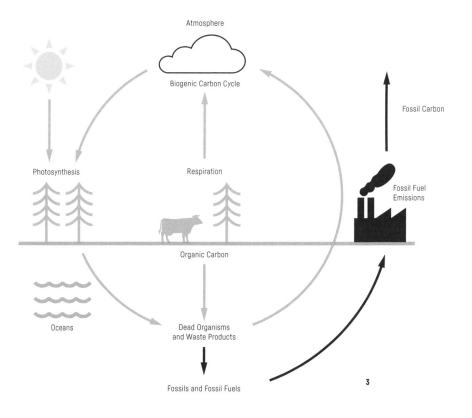

Atmosphere

Biogenic Carbon Cycle

Photosynthesis

Respiration

Fossil Carbon

Fossil Fuel
Emissions

Organic Carbon

Oceans

Dead Organisms
and Waste Products

Fossils and Fossil Fuels

3

4

6

5

1 Helicopter dropping water during a forest fire
2 Forest fire in Canada   **3** The carbon cycle
4 Fossil fuel emissions   **5** Insect infestation:
the brown trees have been attacked by mountain pine
beetles, Canada.   **6** Storm damaged trees, Canada

Sustainable Forest Management

The origins of the term "sustainability" and its guiding principles are to be found in 18th-century European forestry regulations. At the time, early industrialization had generated an increased demand for wood as a building material and an energy source. The mining of metals and salt production required enormous amounts of wood in Germany, Austria, and Switzerland, while coastal countries like Britain, France, Portugal, and Spain were building large numbers of wooden ships in their drives for naval superiority and overseas colonization. Once land had been cleared, it was converted to agricultural use, making forest regrowth impossible.[1] Hans Carl von Carlowitz, a German official who was in charge of ensuring the wood supply for Saxony's mines, became extremely critical of the wasteful and profit-driven attitude toward the use of wood. In his 1713 book *Sylvicultura Oeconomica*, the first comprehensive treatise on forestry, he used the German term *nachhaltend* (sustainable) to promote the conservation and management of forests in an ongoing and sustained manner for the very first time.[2] Over the next two hundred years, his concept of *Nachhaltigkeit,* or sustainability, gradually spread across Europe and to other parts of the world. Not only did his publication serve as the scientific cornerstone of modern forestry, but it also became the foundation of what is known today as sustainable development, which was described in the 1987 Brundtland Report by the United Nations World Commission on Environment and Development as "development that meets the needs of the present without compromising the ability of future generations to meet their own needs."[3]

Historically, sustainability in the realm of traditional forestry has focused mainly on sustainable timber production and meeting economic goals. In recent decades, however, the scope of sustainable forest management has expanded to include broader social, cultural, and environmental objectives.[4] The Food and Agriculture Organization of the United Nations has adopted a definition originally developed by the Ministerial Conference of the Protection of Forests in Europe. Accordingly, sustainable forest management "means the stewardship and use of forests and forest lands in a way, and at a rate, that maintains their biodiversity, productivity, regeneration capacity, vitality and their potential to fulfil, now and in the future, relevant ecological, economic and social functions, at local, national, and global levels, and that does not cause damage to other ecosystems."[5] Within this framework, the primary goal is to achieve a balance between society's ever-increasing needs and the preservation of the world's forests. Sustainable forest management has evolved into a multifaceted and dynamic concept that assigns a variety of functions to forests. These can include timber production, soil and watershed protection, and biodiversity conservation, as well as cultural and recreational purposes.[6] Although many of these purposes are interdependent and can be served simultaneously, multifunctional management adds greater flexibility in responding to varying socioeconomic conditions, environmental contexts, and market trends.[7] Forests are slower to produce a return on investment than are most kinds of agricultural land use and therefore deforestation is often considered the only option for making a living in developing countries. By providing alternative means of generating revenue, sustainable forest management can contribute to green economic development in these parts of the world. Since millions of people living in poverty depend directly on forests for their livelihood, the social commitment of sustainable forest management includes the provision of food, shelter, and medicine for these underprivileged populations, as well as fuel for cooking and heating.[8] Forest-based food production is part of the cultural heritage and traditional knowledge in many countries, and involving indigenous and other local peoples in forest management strategies promotes gender equity, empowers communities, and secures customary rights.[9] In terms of environmental impact, sustainably managed forests can provide greater climate-change mitigation than unmanaged forests can, while simultaneously delivering a range of vital ecological benefits including wildlife habitat, biodiversity conservation, and good water and soil quality.

The practice of controlling the establishment, growth, composition, health, and quality of forests and trees is known as "silviculture."[10] Through various silvicultural practices, foresters influence forest conditions and provide a number of social, economic, and environmental benefits, often mimicking natural disturbances (such as fires, storms, disease outbreaks, and insect infestations) that would occur in an unmanaged forest. Thinning, for example, is a management technique that removes some trees so that the remaining trees have more space to grow, thus reducing competition for sunlight, water, and nutrients. Clearcutting removes all of the trees from a certain area, often leaving patches of trees to serve as wildlife habitat and as buffers alongside streams to protect water and fish. While viewed as controversial by the general public, it is often chosen to promote selected tree species that grow best in full sunlight and therefore cannot compete in mature forests. In addition to thinning and clearcutting, there are regeneration methods that involve partial harvesting. By cutting the majority of trees, a shelterwood system leaves an overstory of maturing trees that allows new trees to grow in a partially shaded microenvironment. Once the new growth is established, the mature overstory trees are typically removed. A group selection system, in contrast, creates a pattern of dispersed openings in the forest, thus promoting the regeneration of various tree species with a range of different shade tolerances. This method produces an uneven-aged forest stand with a high vertical structure that preserves biodiversity and offers a variety of wildlife habitats. Sustainable forest management has to be understood as a dynamic process at all levels, continually responding to new knowledge and adapting to the changing needs and values of society. Ultimately, for its implementation at a global scale to be regarded as successful, it will need to ensure the resilience of the world's forest ecosystems while providing a significant contribution to climate change mitigation.

1 Schmithüsen, Franz. "Three Hundred Years of Applied Sustainability in Forestry." *Unasylva* 64.240 [2013]. 4–5. **2** Grober, Ulrich. *Die Entdeckung der Nachhaltigkeit: Kulturgeschichte eines Begriffs*. Munich: Verlag Antje Kunstmann, 2013. 114–117. **3** *Building Green with Wood: Module 10: Forest Practices in the United States*. ReThink Wood. 3. **4** "Sustainable Forest Management." *Sustainable Forest Management*. Food and Agriculture Organization of the United Nations. Web. 29 Sept. 2015. **5** *RESOLUTION H1: General Guidelines for the Sustainable Management of Forests in Europe*. Helsinki: Second Ministerial Conference on the Protection of Forests in Europe, 1993. 1. **6** "Sustainable Forest Management." Web. 29 Sept. 2015. **7** Schmithüsen, Franz. 11. **8** "SFM for Social Development." *Sustainable Forest Management*. Food and Agriculture Organization of the United Nations. Web. 29 Sept. 2015. **9** "Social Inclusion." *Sustainable Forest Management*. Food and Agriculture Organization of the United Nations. Web. 29 Sept. 2015. **10** "SAFnet Dictionary | Definition For [silviculture]." *SAFnet Dictionary | Definition For [silviculture]*. Society of American Foresters. 30 Sept. 2015.

1 Cover of *Sylvicultura Oeconomica, oder Haußwirthliche Nachricht und Naturmäßige Anweisung zur
Wilden Baum-Zucht,* Hannß Carl von Carlowitz, 1713.
2 Logger 3 Tree harvester

4

4 Loaded logging truck, Canada   **5** Clearcut harvest in Canada mimicking natural disturbances such as fires, storms, disease outbreaks, and insect infestations. Patches of trees retained as wildlife habitats.
6 Group selection harvest in Canada creating a pattern of dispersed openings in the forest. This method produces an uneven-aged forest stand with a high vertical structure that preserves biodiversity and offers a variety of wildlife habitats.

5

6

7

8

9

10

7 Shelterwood system with an overstory of mature
trees that allows new trees to grow in a partially
shaded microenvironment. 8 Reforestation 9 Seed-
lings nursery 10 Young trees in reforested site

Certification Systems

Forest certification supports and complements stewardship efforts and sustainable forest management objectives by ensuring that paper and wood products come from well managed and legally harvested forests.[1] Wood is, in fact, the only structural building material with third-party certification programs in place to verify that products originate from a responsibly managed resource. As a result of increased environmental awareness and growing concern about logging practices and forest degradation, several different certification systems emerged in the 1990s as useful tools for measuring and communicating the economic, environmental, and social impact of forestry practices. Third-party forest certification is a voluntary process in which the procedures and performance of forest operations are evaluated by independent, accredited auditors on the basis of a series of predetermined standards. A team of experts consisting of foresters, biologists, socioeconomists, and other professionals performs the audits on behalf of the certification bodies, which award certificates under their respective programs. Besides the initial certification audit, annual monitoring audits ensure continued conformance to the guidelines of the program concerned.[2]

There are currently more than fifty independent forest certification standards – a fact that reflects the variety of forest types, ecosystems, and ownership structures found around the world. Among these, the *Forest Stewardship Council*® (FSC®) and the *Programme for the Endorsement of Forest Certification* (PEFC) – both international non-governmental organizations – are the two major umbrella certification programs. FSC endorses regional standards based on its international principles and on criteria that are adapted to local conditions. PEFC, in contrast, promotes responsible forest management through the assessment and endorsement of national forest certification schemes. It is the largest certification organization of this kind. Some of the better-known standards recognized by PEFC are those issued by the *Canadian Standards Association* (CSA), the *Sustainable Forestry Initiative* (SFI), and the *American Tree Farm System* (ATFS).[3] While each certification system takes a somewhat different approach to defining principles for sustainable forest management, a variety of standards makes certification more likely, since it makes options available that address regional conditions and the specific needs of individual forest owners.[4] Forest certification is often accompanied by chain of custody certification, which is a mechanism for tracking wood through the supply chain from the point of harvest to its end use, including all the intermediate stages of processing, manufacturing, and distribution. This allows organizations and businesses to verify the origin of the wood in their possession, thus providing evidence that certified material in a certified product originates from certified forests. Many programs also feature trademarks or on-product labeling to demonstrate certification, and these are often employed for marketing purposes.

The world's total certified forest area only accounts for approximately 10 percent of all global forest land today.[5] While certification is intended to improve management practices throughout the world, most certified forestry operations are found in the boreal and temperate forests of Europe and North America. Forest certification in developing countries poses a significant challenge since there is often a lack of awareness and of the capacity to undergo a certification audit and maintain practices to the required standard. The absence of forestry regulations, combined with weak government institutions and ineffective law enforcement mechanisms, exacerbates a situation in which deforestation of valuable tropical forests in these regions is continuing apace. Nevertheless, the proliferation of green building practices and the increased use of biofuels suggest that the worldwide demand for certified wood will continue to grow. It remains to be seen whether the amount of wood available from responsibly and sustainably managed forests will be sufficient to satisfy that demand in the future.[6]

1 *Examining the Linkage Between Forest Regulation and Forest Certification Around the World.* naturally:wood, 2010. 2.   **2** *Building Green with Wood: Module 10: Forest Practices in the United States.* ReThink Wood.   **3** *Wood Specification Green Building Rating System Guides: Certified Wood.* naturally:wood, 2015.   **4** *British Columbia Forest Facts: Third-Party Forest Certification in British Columbia.* naturally:wood, 2013.   **5** Fernholz, Kathryn, Karolina Ehnstrand, Florian Kraxner, Igor Novoselov, Jukka Tissari, and Rupert Oliver. "Policies Shaping Forest Products Markets." *Forest Products Annual Market Review 2013–2014.* Geneva: UNECE, FAO, 2014. 15.   **6** *Vital Forest Graphics.* United Nations Environment Programme, Food and Agriculture Organization of the United Nations, United Nations Forum on Forests, 2009. 55.

1

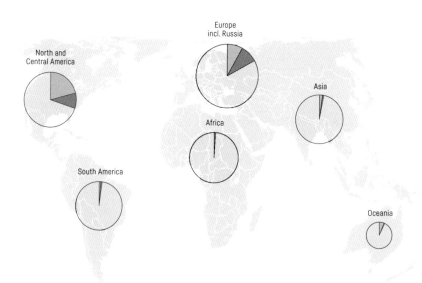

North and
Central America

Europe
incl. Russia

Asia

Africa

South America

Oceania

■ PEFC Certified Forest Area
■ FSC Certified Forest Area
  Non Certified Forest Area

2

3

4

SFI-01669

5

1 Dimensional lumber with PEFC certification stamp   **2** Very little forest area is certified globally **3–7** Logos of the following organizations: Forest Stewardship Council, Programme for the Endorsement of Forest Certification, Sustainable Forestry Initiative, Canadian Standards Association Group – Sustainable Forest Management System, American Tree Farm System

Canadian Sustainable Forest Management

Supporting CSA Z809 –
Canada's SFM Standard

6

7

Forest Products

Among the many raw materials that forests provide, wood is by far the most important renewable resource. For millennia, it was mainly used in its solid form as a building material and an energy source, as well as for making tools, furniture, and other everyday items. Industrialization in the 19th century allowed the mechanical and chemical separation of wood, thus opening up possibilities for the manufacture of thousands of products, ranging from engineered wood to paper, and even to fabric fibers for the textile industry. Today, the large variety of available wood products can broadly be categorized into roundwood, sawnwood, wood-based composite products, pulp and paper products, chemical wood products, and fuel products.

Roundwood represents one of the most efficient uses of wood, since it requires minimal processing between harvesting the tree and marketing the final structural product. Piles, poles, and posts are simply debarked, seasoned, and often treated with preservatives for protection against decay and insect attack.[1] The conversion of logs into dimensional lumber for construction involves sawing members from logs, squaring the edges, and cutting them to length. The resulting sawn softwood or hardwood is available in a number of standard sizes for use as beams, boards, planks, joists, rafters, and other structural elements.[2] Wood-based composite products, also called "engineered wood" products, have mostly been developed in response to faster growth rates, smaller trunk diameters, and the increased proportion of juvenile wood with less strength than mature, slow-growing trees. They are manufactured by combining small-dimensional wood pieces, such as boards, veneers, strands, or fibers, to form large-format products with higher structural design values than those of solid sawn lumber. Plywood, oriented strand board (osb), glued-laminated timber (glulam), laminated veneer lumber (lvl), and cross-laminated timber (clt) are some of the most commonly used engineered wood products. In addition, a significant number of non-structural, composite wood panel products are used in applications such as siding, paneling, cabinetry, and furniture. Other wood-based composites are made by combining wood fibers with materials such as fiberglass, Portland cement, and various kinds of metal or plastic.[3]

Paper and paperboard products are manufactured from wood that has been broken down into a fibrous cellulose pulp, which is then pressed and dried into flexible sheets. Paper is used for communication, storing information, packaging, making sanitary and disposable products, and as a base material for various industrial applications.[4] For many chemical wood products, wood is reduced to its basic chemical components: cellulose, hemicellulose, and lignin. These products find diverse applications as, for example, agents in dyes and paints, ingredients in adhesives and lacquers, and binders in animal feed pellets and textiles. Plastic items such as table-tennis balls and piano keys are molded from cellulose compounds. The set of substances known as "naval stores," including turpentine and rosin, are derived from pine pulp and are used in the manufacture of chemical-based adhesives and coatings such as paints, lacquers, and varnishes.[5] Cellulose wood fiber is used in, among other things, the textile industry to make viscose, a soft, semi-synthetic, regenerated fiber commonly present in clothing, upholstery, drapery, and carpets. It is often considered an alternative to cotton since its production requires less water and land. Regenerated cellulose fibers composed of chemically processed wood cellulose exhibit properties that are more similar to natural fibers such as cotton, flax, hemp, and jute than to nylon and polyester, which are thermoplastic, petroleum-based synthetic fibers.[6] One recently developed fiber with characteristics superior to those of earlier regenerated cellulose fibers is Lyocell (also made from wood pulp), which is, moreover, produced through a more environmentally friendly process.

Wood fuel products include split wood (from roundwood logs) and charcoal, as well as residues such as sawdust, shavings, and chips from logging and sawmill operations. Globally, the primary use of wood today is still as fuel for heating and cooking, with wood fuel production accounting for over 50 percent of the world's total wood harvest. In many developing countries, it often represents the only domestically available and affordable source of energy. While wood fuel is not a primary driver of deforestation at a global scale, it can have negative effects at the local level.[7] Wood fuel use has also increased in the industrialized world in recent years. In an effort to meet the European Union's ambitious 2020 targets, which require that 20 percent of its energy supply comes from renewable sources, many European countries are turning to compressed wood pellets and are granting substantial government subsidies to encourage this. Since Europe does not produce enough timber to meet this additional demand, a large portion of its wood pellet requirement is now being imported from North America, adding to the overall pressure on existing forests and other ecosystems. Production processes and shipping also require a significant amount of energy, which counters the reduction in carbon emissions achieved by switching to wood. The use of wood fuel in itself can be considered carbon-neutral if the wood comes from sustainably managed forests, since harvested areas will be replanted and the same amount of carbon dioxide that is emitted through combustion will be reabsorbed by new tree growth.[8] High upfront carbon emissions, the slow regeneration of forests, and the long-term capture of carbon have stirred public debate about the real immediate benefits of wood biomass energy, in particular since the associated carbon-debt forecasts are based on assumptions about future forest regrowth that are very uncertain in the contexts of climate change and increasing demand on forests worldwide.[9] Considering the long-term impact, however, energy generation from responsibly sourced wood fuel is preferable to the use of fossil fuels, since fossil fuel combustion removes carbon from ancient storage, creating a carbon debt that cannot be balanced on anything less than a geological time scale.[10]

Forest plantations are often established by government authorities or private businesses to meet the growing demand for wood products. They are typically large-scale, actively managed operations that grow wood as even-aged monocultures for the commercial production of timber, wood fuel, raw materials for panel products, and pulpwood for cellulose and paper manufacturing. The wood yield of a plantation forest is generally higher than that of a natural forest since the focus is on the cultivation of fast-growing trees. Compared to temperate species that generally need sixty to one hundred and fifty years to mature, tropical pine and teak are on an approximate twenty-year rotation cycle. Industrial hardwoods such as eucalyptus and acacia can even be harvested less than ten years after planting. Due to their high productivity, forest plantations can help to reduce the pressure on natural forests for wood production. However, there is concern that old-growth forests are being replaced by plantations – a trend that is particularly apparent in the tropical regions, since the local climate is well suited to fast tree growth, land is affordable, and wages are low. This increase in fast-wood plantations can have adverse impacts on biodiversity and soil fertility, and it can result in a loss of revenue sources for indigenous populations that depend on forests for their livelihood.[11]

Besides wood, forests provide a number of important non-timber forest products (NTFP), which may be commodities, substances, or materials obtained from the forest that do not require the harvesting of trees.[12] These include food products (nuts, fruits, seeds, edible fungi, oils, sap syrups, spices, etc.), industrial plant oils, natural pigments, plant gums and resins, barks, fibers, foliage, plant-based insecticides, latex, cork, and medicinal plants. Many of these also serve as raw materials for the pharmaceutical, cosmetic, agricultural, and food industries.[13] While the harvesting of non-timber forest products is widespread around the world, their purpose varies depending on the socioeconomic and ecological context. People use them for subsistence, the maintenance of cultural traditions, spiritual purposes, health and well-being, and as a supplementary or even main source of income. The trade in non-timber forest products has notable economic value, but since many of them are often distributed directly or marketed informally to final customers, it is difficult to estimate their contribution to regional or national economies. Many governments, development agencies, and non-governmental organizations (NGOs) promote the production and sale of NTFPS as a means of encouraging the alleviation of poverty, the development of local markets, and the conservation of cultural and biological diversity, while supplementing sustainable forestry practices.[14] NTFPS can also be produced in various forms of agroforestry, a land-use management system that intentionally integrates trees and shrubs into crop and animal farming. By taking advantage of the mutual benefits offered by the interaction of agriculture and forestry, this method contributes to the creation of diverse, productive, and sustainable integrated land-use systems.[15]

1 *Wood Handbook: Wood as an Engineering Material.* Madison, WI: United States Department of Agriculture, Forest Service, Forest Products Laboratory, 2010: 6–1.　**2** Bowyer, Jim L., Rubin Shmulsky, and John G. Haygreen. *Forest Products and Wood Science: An Introduction.* 5th ed. Ames, IA: Blackwell, 2007. 321.　**3** Bowyer, Jim L., Rubin Shmulsky, and John G. Haygreen. 353, 383.　**4** Bowyer, Jim L., Rubin Shmulsky, and John G. Haygreen. 435.　**5** Bowyer, Jim L., Rubin Shmulsky, and John G. Haygreen. 476–478.　**6** Mass, Ed. "Rayon, Modal, and Tencel – Environmental Friends or Foes." *YesItsOrganic.com.* Web. 21 Apr. 2016.　**7** *Criteria and Indicators for Sustainable Woodfuels.* Rome: Food and Agriculture Organization of the United Nations, 2010. 3–5.　**8** "The Fuel of the Future." *The Economist,* 06 Apr. 2013. Web. 28 Oct. 2015.　**9** Ernsting, Almuth. *Sustainable Biomass: A Modern Myth.* Biofuelwatch, 2012. 30.　**10** Bowyer, Jim, Steve Bratkovich, Matt Frank, Jeff Howe, Sarah Stai, and Kathryn Fernholz. *Carbon 101: Understanding the Carbon Cycle and the Forest Carbon Debate.* Minneapolis: Dovetail Partners, 2012. 11.　**11** *Vital Forest Graphics.* United Nations Environment Programme, Food and Agriculture Organization of the United Nations, United Nations Forum on Forests, 2009. 24–25.　**12** "Glossary of Forestry Terms in British Columbia." *Ministry of Forests and Range Library.* British Columbia Ministry of Forests and Range, Mar. 2008. Web. 28 Oct. 2015.　**13** *Green Economy and Trade: Trends, Challenges and Opportunities.* Geneva: United Nations Environment Programme, 2013. 132.　**14** "Forests and Non-timber Forest Products." *Forests and Non-timber Forest Products.* Center for International Forestry Research. Web. 29 Oct. 2015.　**15** "Agroforestry Practices." *Agroforestry Practices.* USDA National Agroforestry Center. Web. 29 Oct. 2015.

1

1 Unloading of roundwood, Switzerland
2 Roundwood   3 Sawnwood, Switzerland
4 Engineered wood products: plywood, oriented
strand board, glued-laminated timber, and I-joist

2

3

4

5

6

7

8

9

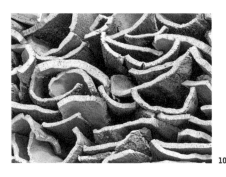

10

5 Wood fuel: chips   **6** Wood fuel: pellets
7 Pine forest plantation   **8** Agroforestry: coffee
plantation under forest canopy   **9** Non-timber
forest product: extraction of latex for use in rubber
production   **10** Non-timber forest product: cork bark

Carbon Sequestration and Substitution Potential

As previously explained, forests serve as carbon pools since trees absorb carbon during their growth and store it for many years. This long-term capture of atmospheric carbon dioxide is called "carbon sequestration." The carbon does not get released back into the atmosphere naturally until the trees die and decay or are consumed in a wildfire. However, when trees are harvested to produce wood, the building materials or products made from this wood continue to store carbon as long as they exist, effectively creating a carbon pool in the form of long-lived wood products. A timber building will therefore keep the carbon captured in its wood out of the atmosphere for the lifetime of the structure. In a sustainably managed forest, each log that is utilized also makes room for new trees to grow, with the opportunity to sequester more carbon from the atmosphere.

Wood is produced through the process of photosynthesis with the use of solar energy, and very little additional energy is needed to transform it into usable building products. Compared with products made from non-renewable materials, wood products contain relatively little embodied energy, which is the energy expended over a product's entire life cycle, including its manufacture, transport, use, and final disposal. The energy required to manufacture finished wood products is generally less than half of the amount that is stored in them.[1] This process is far less dependent on fossil fuels than the manufacturing of many other building products is, especially since the forest industry generates much of its own energy through the combustion of mill residues including sawdust and tree bark, as well as by-products of pulping from papermaking. Most wood products can easily be reused or recycled at the end of their service life. Alternatively, the energy stored in the wood can serve as a carbon-neutral source for the generation of heating energy or electricity.

The low consumption of energy in production and the limited use of fossil fuel-derived energy mean that wood products typically cause much lower carbon dioxide emissions than functionally comparable products.[2] Substituting wood for energy- and carbon-intensive materials such as aluminum, steel, concrete, and brick in long-term applications can therefore result in substantial carbon benefits, which accumulate over time.[3] Several life-cycle assessment studies completed in recent years demonstrate that buildings made of wood require the least energy in comparison with those constructed of other conventional building materials.[4] Since a large portion of the material used in a building is attributable to its structural system, using wood for the primary structure can significantly reduce energy consumption, in particular fossil fuel energy consumption and any associated emissions of fossil carbon.[5]

Concern regarding the impact of construction on the global climate is growing worldwide, and the environmental benefits of making buildings that minimize energy consumption during their operation – with correspondingly low operating costs – have already been recognized by the general public. As higher-performance, more energy-efficient buildings have been developed, the need to reduce their embodied energy becomes more apparent, since it makes up a considerable portion of the building's total energy use over its life cycle.[6] Although wood is not necessarily the appropriate choice for all applications, there are clear environmental advantages to using it wherever possible, as long as it is obtained from responsibly managed sources. A healthy demand for wood products also encourages landowners to keep their land forested, avoiding large-scale carbon losses to the atmosphere through land use changes.[7] While much work remains to be done to reduce deforestation and forest degradation – particularly in the tropical regions – substituting wood for building materials that consume large amounts of energy derived from fossil fuels could prove to be a viable strategy for mitigating climate change and achieving 'green' economic development.

1 *Bauen mit Holz = Aktiver Klimaschutz.* Munich: Holzforschung München, Technische Universität München, 2010. 6–8.   2 Bowyer, Jim, Steve Bratkovich, Matt Frank, Jeff Howe, Sarah Stai, and Kathryn Fernholz. *Carbon 101: Understanding the Carbon Cycle and the Forest Carbon Debate.* Minneapolis: Dovetail Partners, 2012. 8.   3 Oliver, Chadwick Dearing, Nedal T. Nassar, Bruce R. Lippke, and James B. McCarter. "Carbon, Fossil Fuel, and Biodiversity Mitigation With Wood and Forests." *Journal of Sustainable Forestry* 33.3 (2014). 248.   4 Bowyer, Jim, Steve Bratkovich, Alison Lindburg, and Kathryn Fernholz. *Wood Products and Carbon Protocols: Carbon Storage and Low Energy Intensity Should Be Considered.* Minneapolis, MN: Dovetail Partners, 2008. 4.   5 Bowyer, Jim, Steve Bratkovich, Matt Frank, Jeff Howe, Sarah Stai, and Kathryn Fernholz. 8; Mayo, Joseph. *Solid Wood.* New York: Routledge, 2015. 10.   6 *Bauen mit Holz = Aktiver Klimaschutz.* 10.   7 Ward, Roxane, and Dave Patterson. *The Impact of Wood Use on North American Forests.* ReThink Wood, 2015. 7.

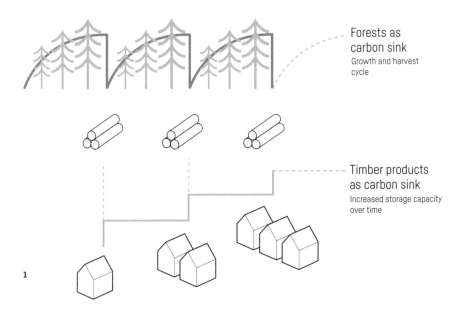

Forests as carbon sink
Growth and harvest cycle

Timber products as carbon sink
Increased storage capacity over time

1

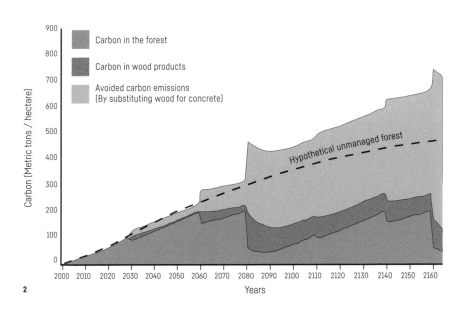

2

3

4

5

1 Carbon storage of wood products   **2** Substitution potential of wood products   **3** Managed forests sequester carbon from the atmosphere   **4** Long-lived wood products as carbon sinks: cross-laminated timber panels   **5** Wood is used for the primary structural system instead of steel or concrete. Whitmore Road, London. Architect: Waugh Thistleton Architects. Engineer: Akera Engineers.

Industry and Wood Utilization

While deforestation and forest degradation are causing an ongoing reduction of forest land in the tropical regions, the forest stock in the industrialized countries of North America and Europe is increasing. Timber growth in the managed forests of these countries continues to exceed removals and has done so for the last several decades. Harvest rates currently average around 60 to 65 percent of new forest growth, resulting in a net increase of inventory.[1] Additionally, only a very small percentage of the standing tree stock is removed each year. In the United States, for example, only around 1.3 percent of all forest land is affected by annual harvests, while in Germany it is even less at about 0.2 percent, which is well below the maximum levels deemed sustainable.[2]

Wood removed from forests can now be processed extremely efficiently by sawmills and other manufacturing facilities, leaving almost no waste. Over the last seventy-five years, the forest products sector in the developed nations has made remarkable progress towards becoming a zero-waste industry by developing new products and investing in innovative manufacturing technologies. This has significantly reduced its environmental impact. In the 1940s, the yield of sawn lumber from logs entering mills was approximately 35 to 39 percent, with a resulting waste volume of 50 to 60 percent. While a portion of the waste was used for generating energy and heating, most of it was incinerated or landfilled. Efficiency increased considerably after World War II, when sawmill residues began being used in papermaking processes and for the production of particleboard. The computerization of mill operations in the 1970s introduced electronic scanning, evaluation, and the precise positioning of logs during cutting, which optimized trimming processes and improved lumber yield. Technological innovations led to advances in plywood manufacturing and allowed the development of new structural composite lumber and panel products such as laminated veneer lumber (LVL) and oriented strand board (OSB). These new processing techniques enabled the economical use of small-diameter, low-strength trees in the manufacture of large-format, high-strength products that had previously required large-diameter logs, thus raising lumber yields to 41 percent by the mid-1980s. More stringent environmental legislation, in combination with the 1973 oil crisis, motivated many sawmills to reduce their reliance on fossil fuels by increasing the use of wood waste to produce their own heat and energy.[3] Today, biofuels – in the form of mill residues, logging residuals, and small-diameter trees from forest thinning – ensure near self-sufficiency of the forest products industry by providing about 70 percent of its energy needs.[4] Many manufacturing facilities produce both heat and power from wood fuels by employing cogeneration equipment, which is far more efficient than conventional energy-generation systems, thus reducing greenhouse gas emissions. Although the combustion of woody biomass in place of fossil fuels still releases carbon dioxide, it causes biogenic carbon emissions that are part of the natural cycle and are offset by new tree growth.[5] Since the beginning of the 21st century, ongoing efforts to improve technology and increase yield have resulted in lumber yields of 52 percent with virtually no waste. Logs entering sawmills and manufacturing centers are almost entirely converted into usable products. By fully utilizing mill residues that had previously gone unused, the forest products industry has managed to create zero-waste facilities. The next step will be to expand the reuse, recycling, and recovery of wood products at the end of their service life.[6]

1 *Forest Europe, 2015: State of Europe's Forests 2015.* Madrid: Ministerial Conference on the Protection of Forests in Europe, 2015. 117; *National Report on Sustainable Forests - 2010.* United States Department of Agriculture, Forest Service, 2011. II–40; "National Forestry Database (NFD)." *National Forestry Database (NFD).* Web. 10 Nov. 2015.   **2** *Trend Data.* Forest Service: Forest Inventory and Analysis National Program. Web. 10 Nov. 2015; *Der Wald in Deutschland: Ausgewählte Ergebnisse der dritten Bundeswaldinventur.* Berlin: Bundesministerium für Ernährung und Landwirtschaft, 2014. 29–38.   **3** Bowyer, Jim, Steve Bratkovich, and Kathryn Fernholz. *Utilization of Harvested Wood by the North American Forest Products Industry.* Minneapolis, MN: Dovetail Partners, 2012. 2–6.   **4** Bowyer, Jim, Steve Bratkovich, Matt Frank, Jeff Howe, Sarah Stai, and Kathryn Fernholz. *Carbon 101: Understanding the Carbon Cycle and the Forest Carbon Debate.* Minneapolis: Dovetail Partners, 2012. 9.   **5** Miner, Reid. *Impact of the Global Forest Industry on Atmospheric Greenhouse Gases.* Rome: Food and Agriculture Organization of the United Nations, 2010. 5.   **6** Bowyer, Jim, Steve Bratkovich, and Kathryn Fernholz. 6–8.

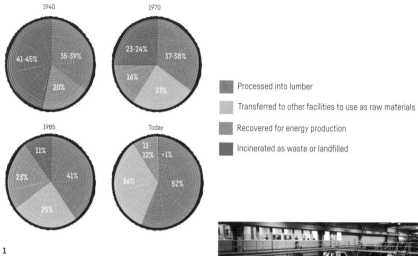

1940   1970

1985   Today

41-45%   35-39%   20%

23-24%   37-38%   16%   23%

11%   23%   41%   25%

11-12%   <1%   36%   52%

■ Processed into lumber

□ Transferred to other facilities to use as raw materials

▨ Recovered for energy production

▦ Incinerated as waste or landfilled

1

2

3

4

5

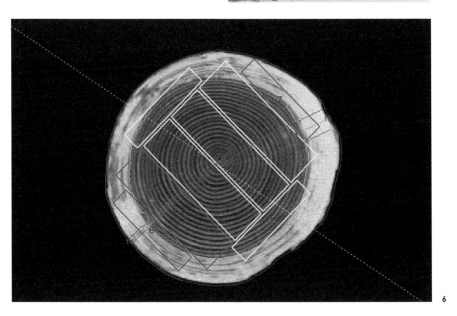

6

7

1 Utilization of harvested wood by the North American forest products industry   **2** Lumber mill   **3** Lumber grading   **4** Solid-sawn lumber   **5** X-ray scanning allows grading of logs for subsequent breakdown, bucking, and sorting   **6** Digitized cutting pattern optimization   **7** Computed tomography (CT) allows full 3D log reconstruction to locate internal defects for optimized sawing

Reuse and Recycling

Each log that is harvested from a responsibly managed forest allows another tree to grow in its place, which makes wood a truly renewable building material. The same cannot be said of other construction materials such as aluminum, steel, concrete, and plastic. Their global supply of raw materials is limited, and their energy-intensive manufacture relies on fossil fuels that are equally limited. The substitution of these materials with wood products can have a substantial impact on the long-term reserves of natural resources available to future generations on the Earth.[1]

As already noted, by maximizing the utilization of raw wood materials, the forest products industry has been very effective in reducing the amount of waste it creates. This has been largely achieved through pre-consumer waste-recycling, which means that any wood waste accumulated during the manufacturing process is diverted from the waste stream and recycled into other products, or incinerated for on-site energy generation. Products with high pre-consumer recycled wood content include particleboard, fiberboard, oriented strand board (OSB), and parallel strand lumber (PSL).[2] As a result of these successful zero-waste efforts, the industry has now shifted its focus to the reduction of post-consumer waste, which involves recycling materials and consumer products discarded by households and commercial, industrial, and institutional facilities at the end of their useful life. Certain products such as hardwood flooring, heavy timbers, framing lumber, railroad ties, and pallets are already frequently recycled, but significant volumes of wood waste are still generated as Municipal Solid Waste (MSW) and Construction and Demolition (C&D) waste. In order to promote increased recovery from these streams, some regions have established regulations that no longer permit landfilling of wood. While additional opportunities to expand post-consumer wood recycling do exist, these efforts will ultimately require commitment by the forest products industry to identify and encourage best practices for wood recovery in support of waste reduction and diversion.

One strategy for improvement is to prevent wood from entering the waste stream by retaining it at manufacturing facilities where reuse and recycling protocols are in place. To this effect, an integrated approach to building design, involving the architect, the engineer, the manufacturer, and the contractor, could increase the degree to which building components are prefabricated, thus minimizing on-site construction waste. Furthermore, using mechanical fasteners and avoiding adhesives could facilitate end-of-life disassembly and material recovery. This would promote the deconstruction of wood buildings rather than conventional demolition and landfill practices. Manufacturing centers could provide labeled, cut-to-length framing lumber directly to builders and secondary processors instead of supplying dimensional lumber in standard lengths, keeping any cut-off waste at the factory. Voluntary take-back programs of the kind commonly found in the office furniture, automobile, and electronics industries could demonstrate that forest products manufacturers are willing to take responsibility for the entire life cycle of their products, including recycling and final disposal.[3]

Wood is not recycled in the same manner as many other recyclable materials such as paper, aluminum cans, and glass bottles, which are generally used as feedstock for the manufacture of similar consumer products. Rather, wood tends to be removed from buildings through deconstruction practices, which allows the material to be reused in another form. This reclamation of waste wood has become a new source of raw materials for the building industry and has generated a specialty market for niche products. Heavy timbers from historic buildings, for example, are frequently remanufactured into flooring, siding, or wall paneling.[4] Reclaimed wood products often consist of wood that was originally harvested from primary forests several hundred years ago, which is appreciated for its unique appearance and its superior strength, stability, and durability compared with newly sawn wood. The reuse of old-growth lumber diverts valuable building materials from the waste stream, extends their carbon storage benefits, and reduces the environmental impact of sourcing and manufacturing new products.[5]

While post-consumer recycling is already common in the case of some wood products, there is still plenty of room to improve the degree of material recovery. Successful initiatives are likely to involve technological innovation and the establishment of new partnerships between industry, municipalities, and building professionals, as well as the promotion of wood as a renewable material that is well suited to green construction. The fact that many green building programs and certification standards recognize the environmental advantages of recycled and reclaimed wood products might serve as an added incentive for their increased use in the future.[6]

1 Bowyer, Jim, Steve Bratkovich, Matt Frank, Jeff Howe, Sarah Stai, and Kathryn Fernholz. *Carbon 101: Understanding the Carbon Cycle and the Forest Carbon Debate.* Minneapolis: Dovetail Partners, 2012. 10.   2 *Green Building Rating System Guides: Wood Specification: Recycled Materials.* ReThink Wood, 2014.   3 Howe, Jeff, Steve Bratkovich, Jim Bowyer, Matt Frank, and Kathryn Fernholz. *The Current State of Wood Reuse and Recycling in North America and Recommendations for Improvements.* Minneapolis, MN: Dovetail Partners, 2013. 4–9.   4 Howe, Jeff, Steve Bratkovich, Jim Bowyer, Matt Frank, and Kathryn Fernholz. 7, 41.   5 Bratkovich, Steve, Jim Bowyer, Alison Lindburg, and Kathryn Fernholz. *Reclaiming Lumber Products from Waste Wood.* Minneapolis, MN: Dovetail Partners, 2009. 2–3.   6 Bratkovich, Steve, Jim Bowyer, Alison Lindburg, and Kathryn Fernholz. 10–11.

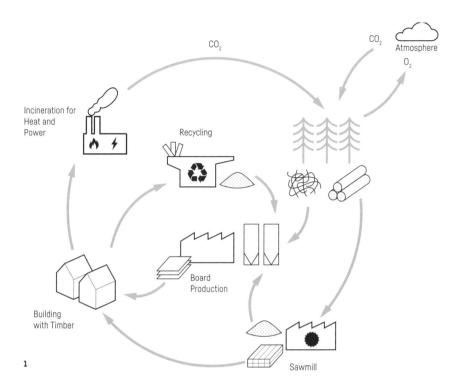

CO$_2$

CO$_2$

Atmosphere

O$_2$

Incineration for
Heat and
Power

Recycling

Building
with Timber

Board
Production

Sawmill

1

3

2

4

5

6

1 Use and recycling of wood products   **2** Post-consumer wood waste   **3** High pre-consumer recycled content: oriented strand board (OSB) manufacturing **4 + 5** Prefabrication of building components in the shop minimizes on-site construction waste   **6** Demolishing of barn for wood reclamation

Life-Cycle Assessment

As the pressure to lower carbon emissions grows, building designers are increasingly turning to sustainable construction practices in order to reduce the carbon footprint of buildings. While it is crucial to follow the recommendations of
voluntary rating programs, many model building codes are also beginning to
include green building provisions. Wood can play a critical role in these efforts
since it possesses a number of environmental advantages over other building
materials, most importantly recyclability, renewability, and lower levels of embodied energy.

The benefits of using wood are recognized and rewarded by green building rating
systems, but early initiatives based their evaluation mainly on extensive lists of
prescriptive standards for reducing energy consumption and various environmental impacts. Each recommended or required measure typically addressed a
single attribute such as the usage of third-party certified wood, the incorporation of recycled, reused, and salvaged products, local sourcing and the efficient
use of materials, the minimization of waste, and improved indoor air quality.[1]
While most green building programs continue to rely on these types of provisions today, the recommendations for the use of wood tend to vary widely
among the various systems, making an objective assessment difficult. In recent
years, many rating systems have therefore moved away from solely employing prescriptive measures and are instead relying on the systematic performance-based evaluation of materials, assemblies, and entire buildings by
means of life-cycle assessment (LCA).[2]

Life-cycle assessment studies are the most comprehensive tool for determining the
full environmental impact of building materials and products over their entire
life cycle, from the extraction or harvest of raw materials through manufacturing, transportation, installation, use, and maintenance, to disposal or recycling.[3]
This science-based method involves quantifying all of the relevant material and
energy flows throughout the life of a product, either as inputs or outputs, and
assessing their conceivable environmental effects. The indicators that are typically measured include global warming potential, ozone depletion potential,
resource consumption, acidification and eutrophication potential, waste generation, and water usage.[4] All of the LCA data generated must adhere to a set of
guidelines provided by the International Organization for Standardization (ISO),
thus allowing the direct and objective comparison of any benefits and tradeoffs.
The evaluation of an entire building can be a costly and complicated process
since it entails analyzing all of the assemblies, subassemblies, and individual
components. Fortunately, a growing number of life-cycle assessment tools are
available to building designers at little or no cost. These provide detailed environmental impact information for a wide range of generic building assembly
configurations, with the option for users to add their own materials and custom

products to the database. Upon defining the structural and envelope assemblies, the designer is provided with a life-cycle inventory of the entire building, enabling a quick and easy comparison of multiple design options. While LCA tools recognize materials with low CO_2 emissions, they do not take into account the long-term storage capacity of carbon, which is one of wood's unique benefits.[5] Several organizations offer carbon calculators, which provide an estimate of the amount of carbon stored in a wood building and of the greenhouse gas emissions that could be avoided by substituting wood for steel and concrete.[6]

Some of the major green building rating systems and model building codes also recognize and encourage the use of Environmental Product Declarations (EPDs). EPDS are standardized, independently verified reports on the environmental performance of products, materials, and services. They are based on life-cycle assessment and have worldwide validity because they conform to ISO standards. An EPD presents relatively complex information about product attributes and manufacturing impacts in a neutral, concise, and consistent way, thus simplifying building product choices and comparisons for industrial customers and end-use consumers. Producing an EPD can be expensive and may require manufacturers to disclose information that might be considered confidential, but many in the building industry are beginning to see the advantages of furnishing verifiable and comprehensive environmental data for their products, since it demonstrates a commitment to sustainability and stewardship. However, EPDS are not the only measure of a product's environmental attributes and impacts. In the case of wood products, sustainable forest management certification incorporates parameters not contained in an EPD, including fair practices, biodiversity conservation, soil and water quality, and the protection of wildlife habitat. EPDs and forest certification therefore complement each other by providing a more complete picture of a product's environmental performance. The use of Environmental Product Declarations in the building industry is expanding, due to the growing demand for more sustainable building practices and the resulting need for greater transparency. Europe, Asia, and Australia have been playing a leading role in the development of EPDs, with North America following closely behind.

While life-cycle assessment does not address every concern, it has emerged as the most comprehensive tool for evaluating and comparing building products on the basis of key environmental impacts.[7] The shift from a prescriptive approach to sustainable design toward systematic, performance-based considerations is allowing designers, builders, and consumers to make informed decisions about the products they specify and use. LCA comparisons of equivalent buildings, assemblies, and components consistently demonstrate that wood performs better over its life cycle than alternative materials in terms of embodied energy, greenhouse gas emissions, air and water pollution, and other impact indicators.

These environmental advantages are likely to ensure that the use of wood products will continue to increase in the future for a variety of applications, making an essential contribution to the development of more sustainable buildings.[8]

1 *Green Building and Wood Products: Increasing Recognition of Wood's Environmental Advantages.* ReThink Wood, 2015. 1–4.   2 *Green Building Rating System Guides: Wood Specification: Life Cycle Assessment.* ReThink Wood, 2014. 2.   3 "Life Cycle Assessment." *Life Cycle Assessment.* naturally:wood. Web. 24 Nov. 2015.   4 *Green Building Rating System Guides: Wood Specification: Life Cycle Assessment.* 1.   5 *Green Building and Wood Products: Increasing Recognition of Wood's Environmental Advantages.* 5–7.   6 Ward, Roxane, and Dave Patterson. *The Impact of Wood Use on North American Forests.* ReThink Wood, 2015. 5.   7 Evans, Layne. *Wood and Environmental Product Declarations.* ReThink Wood, American Wood Council, Canadian Wood Council, 2013. 1–6.   8 *Green Building and Wood Products: Increasing Recognition of Wood's Environmental Advantages.* 5–8.

Resource Extraction

Manufacturing

Recycling, Reuse,
Disposal

On-Site
Construction

Demolition

Occupancy /
Maintenance

1

1 Life cycle of building products   **2 + 3** The benefits of
using wood are recognized and rewarded by many
green building rating systems. UBC Earth Sciences
Building, Vancouver, BC. Architect: Perkins + Will.
Engineer: Equilibrium Consulting.

2

3

4

4 Meredith Center Arena, Chelsea, Québec. Architect:
Martin Marcotte/Beinhaker Architects. Engineer: Nordic
Structures, SDK and Associates.   **5** Surrey Central
City, Surrey, BC. Architect: Bing Thom Architects.
Engineer: StructureCraft.   **6** EPD summary brief for
North American Laminated Veneer Lumber by the
American Wood Council and Canadian Wood Council
7 Great Eastern Buildings, London. Architect: Kara-
kusevic Carson Architects. Engineer: Price & Myers.
8 + 9 Excerpt from the Environmental Product Declara-
tion (EPD) for North American Glued Laminated Timbers
by the American Wood Council and Canadian Wood
Council

5

6

7

8

9

Globalization Trends

As is the case with many other industries, globalization has drastically affected the manufacture of forest products in recent years. Traditionally, the forest industry was dependent on raw wood that was sourced locally from natural forest stands. Since wood was harvested at high volumes, but was of relatively low value, the transportation of logs generated considerable costs, often resulting in processing facilities being located nearby. The manufacture of pulp, lumber, and finished products therefore occurred close to forest land, with subsequent transportation to key market areas. Regions with abundant timber resources were able to benefit from employment opportunities as well as revenue streams generated by the primary and secondary forest products sectors, which allowed any added value to be retained locally.[1] Throughout the 20th century and continuing today, 75 percent of all industrial roundwood intended for further processing into products has been harvested in the developed countries of North America, Europe, and Oceania – regions that have also dominated the wood products manufacturing sector. In comparison, the developing countries only accounted for about 25 percent of the industrial wood harvest during the same period. Although they are responsible for 90 percent of global wood fuel production, these nations have played only a marginal role in the forest products sector.[2] However, recent developments related to globalization, third-world economic growth, and technological innovation seem to indicate that the worldwide patterns of wood harvesting, forest products manufacturing, and consumption are changing.[3]

Forest-sector activities are shifting from the temperate, industrialized nations that possess vast timber resources and long-established wood products industries to tropical, mostly developing regions with no history of significant forest products production. These emerging economies offer competitive manufacturing conditions with lower labor and land costs, as well as favorable climates that support fast-growing planted forests with higher yields. Capitalizing on the cost advantages of these particular regions has resulted not only in the outsourcing of jobs and the redirection of capital investment and technology, but most significantly, the relocation of the forest itself as a resource. Fifty years ago, nearly all roundwood was harvested from natural forests, but these are gradually being replaced by intensively managed forest plantations as the main source of wood supplies.[4] Plantation forests make up less than 7 percent of the world's forest area today, but they account for approximately 34 percent of global industrial roundwood production. Current estimates predict that this will increase to over 50 percent by 2050.[5] The continued improvement of wood-based composite products has reduced the need for large-diameter trees by providing suitable substitutes for large, structural, solid-sawn, lumber products. The ability to use small-diameter trees for a wide range of products reduces the incentives for long-rotation forest management and encourages the further development of rapid-growth industrial wood plantations.[6] Although some highly productive planted pine forests can be found in the southern United States, the majority of these new monocultures of conifers, eucalyptus, acacia, or other species are located in the developing nations of Asia and the southern hemisphere.[7] They typically consist of a large number of even-aged trees of the same species, which are bred for fast growth, uniformity, and a high yield of raw material. Despite the potential of intensively managed forest plantations to satisfy the growing worldwide demand for wood, there is substantial controversy over their expansion, since they are sometimes established by converting natural forests and can additionally cause negative effects on plant and animal biodiversity.[8]

Besides the increase of wood supplies from tropical plantation forests, large quantities of industrial roundwood have come onto the world market in connection with the recovery of Russia's forest and wood products sector, which collapsed after the breakup of the Soviet Union in the 1990s. With vast wood resources, it is now re-emerging with increased harvest levels and exports of industrial roundwood, expecting to contribute significantly to global lumber supply in the future. China and other countries with emerging economies have increased their imports of logs and lumber from nations with abundant timber resources such as Russia and the United States in order to satisfy the input demands of their wood products industries. Many of the secondary products manufactured from these wood supplies (including furniture, flooring, and plywood panels) are subsequently marketed in developed countries at prices well below those of domestic producers.[9] The close proximity of manufacturing facilities to forest resources is no longer critical since the cost of transporting logs or finished products over long distances is essentially offset by the low cost of processing.[10] As the consumer base in the industrializing countries expands, rapidly growing demand for wood products will likely lead to reduced exports of goods and increased imports of raw materials.[11] Significant capital investment in the production facilities of these new wood-producing regions will stimulate an expansion of their industrial capacities. Considering the current cost advantages, their forest products industries will continue to gain global market share, ultimately requiring a rethinking of established business strategies and product lines in the developed countries.

Globalization trends and international competition will continue to move manufacturing activity to emerging economies by allowing the flow of capital and technology to regions with low labor costs, while simultaneously opening up new markets for wood products. The shift of the forest sector to tropical developing countries will certainly affect forest certification programs, since the temperate developed regions account for the majority of the world's certified forests today.[12] Most significantly, rapid-growth forest plantations will be instrumental in the provision of future wood supplies and are projected to become a critical form of industrial forestry development over the coming decades.[13]

1 Sedjo, Roger A., and David Bael. *The Impact of Globalization on the Forest Products Industry.* Pittsburgh, PA: Industry Studies Association, 2007. 1.　**2** Bowyer, Jim L. "Changing Realities in Forest Sector Markets." *Unasylva* 55.219 (2004). 59.　**3** Bowyer, Jim L., Jeff Howe, Phil Guillery, and Kathryn Fernholz. *Trends In The Global Forest Sector And Implications For Forest Certification.* White Bear Lake, MN: Dovetail Partners, 2004. 3.　**4** Bael, David, and Roger Sedjo. *Toward Globalization of the Forest Products Industry.* Washington, DC: Resources for the Future, 2006. 1–6.　**5** *Global Forest Resources Assessment 2015.* Food and Agriculture Organization of the United Nations, 2015. 17–19; Jürgensen, Christian, Walter Kollert und Arvydas Lebedys. *Assessment of Industrial Roundwood Production from Planted Forests. FAO Planted Forests and Trees Working Paper FP/48/E.* Rome: Food and Agriculture Organization of the United Nations, 2014. 4–15.　**6** Bowyer, Jim L. 63.　**7** Bowyer, Jim L., Jeff Howe, Phil Guillery, and Kathryn Fernholz. 3.　**8** Bowyer, Jim L., Rubin Shmulsky, and John G. Haygreen. *Forest Products and Wood Science: An Introduction.* 5th ed. Ames, IA: Blackwell, 2007. 488–489.　**9** Bowyer, Jim L., Jeff Howe, Phil Guillery, and Kathryn Fernholz. 4–6.　**10** *Vital Forest Graphics.* United Nations Environment Programme, Food and Agriculture Organization of the United Nations, United Nations Forum on Forests, 2009. 27–28.　**11** Prestemon, Jeffrey P., David N. Wear, and Michaela O. Foster. *The Global Position of the U.S. Forest Products Industry.* Asheville, NC: USDA Forest Service, 2015. 21.　**12** Bowyer, Jim L. 59–64.　**13** Cossalter, Christian, and Charlie Pye-Smith. *Fast-Wood Forestry: Myths and Realities.* Jakarta: Center for International Forestry Research, 2003. 45.

1

2

1 Boreal forest, Russia　2 The developed countries have dominated the industrial roundwood market throughout the 20th century. Loaded logging truck, Canada.　3 Industrial roundwood is increasingly shipped to emerging markets for further processing due to low labor costs. Shipping yard, New Zealand. 4 Eucalyptus plantation, Brazil

3

The Carpentry Trade

Wood played a key role in the development of vernacular building styles from pre-
historic times to the beginning of the Industrial Age. Widely available, renewable, and easily worked, it became the construction material of choice for many
cultures around the world. Regionally specific building forms and methods of
construction were determined by the prevailing climatic conditions, customs
and traditions, and the experience and skill set of the local population.

For thousands of years, building depended on the sourcing and processing of locally available materials, of which wood was one of the most versatile, as it could
be adapted to a diverse range of conditions.[1] Ancient Greek and Roman builders erected structures that skillfully demonstrated wood's ability to span long
distances. Nomadic tribes in Africa, Asia, and the Americas employed wood-
en posts in the construction of tents and yurts to meet their need for highly
mobile shelters. Traditional Chinese and Japanese wood architecture became
well known for its elaborate joinery techniques and pagodas, which were built
several stories tall. Timber construction flourished in regions rich with forests,
most notably in Scandinavia, Russia, the Alpine regions, and Central Europe.
Beginning in the Roman era, through the Gothic period, and into the early 20th
century, the construction of wood formwork for concrete and masonry arches
and vaults required a high degree of workmanship. As the knowledge and skills
of working with wood evolved and were passed down from one generation to
the next, carpentry became established as one of the oldest and most important building trades. Carpenters were not only competent craftsmen, but they
also emerged as master builders, with a role comparable to the architect and
structural engineer in one. The use of wood for construction over centuries led
to the development and refinement of a tectonic language that would serve as
a basis for many other building materials. Later steel and concrete construction
techniques would borrow heavily from the structural logic of traditional timber
framing.[2]

As the population and density of cities around the world grew, recurring fires
caused severe devastation and loss of life, resulting in the enactment of new
regulations that limited the use of wood in construction. Nevertheless, wood
continued to be employed extensively in urban centers up to the 19th century,
until new processing techniques for iron, steel, and concrete were introduced
in the Industrial Age. These materials facilitated the construction of innovative
structures that offered greater height, permanence, non-combustibility, and improved comfort in comparison with timber buildings. Whereas building with
wood had always been tied to a specific location, advancements in transportation meant that building materials could now be shipped inexpensively over
great distances, regardless of their origin. Wood's decline was furthered by
the emergence of modern architectural styles that promoted the use of mass-

produced components made of steel, glass, and concrete, often to achieve a universal aesthetic. Wood was increasingly marginalized as a low-cost, low-quality building material only utilized by the rural population, and its use in construction declined sharply.[3] As a result, the broad range of responsibility that the carpenter had previously held as the master builder on the jobsite also diminished. A shortage of raw materials in the late 1920s and early 1930s, as well as during the two world wars, briefly led to an increased demand for wood in the construction and manufacturing industries. However, this quickly subsided when the focus of attention returned to steel and concrete in the post-war years.[4] Timber construction finally experienced a resurgence in the late 20th century, when a number of young architects in Europe – mainly in Switzerland, Germany, and Austria – began reviving age-old techniques that would serve as a foundation for new developments and innovations in the field.[5] In their pursuit of a new formal language, they sought inspiration both in the local vernacular architecture and in traditions of high-quality craftsmanship. These architects succeeded in reestablishing wood as a material that could successfully meet the stringent requirements imposed on buildings today, thus offering an alternative to other types of construction. Carpenters, in particular, benefited from this change, since they regained the responsibility for the construction of entire buildings after decades of having been relegated to the mere installation of roof structures.[6]

Today, many carpenters work in close collaboration with architects and structural engineers as integral partners and play an active role in the planning and design process. The traditional carpentry shop has gone beyond manual methods of fabrication and has successfully made the transition to modern, computer-assisted design and production processes. The use of modular building systems, high levels of prefabrication, and efficient equipment for transportation and lifting has streamlined off-site manufacturing and facilitates rapid and precise installation on site. At times, joint ventures between smaller businesses and larger industrial manufacturers are established for sizable construction projects in order to combine high standards of workmanship with increased production capacities. The continued development of wood-based composite products, hybrid construction systems, and modern fasteners has opened up significant markets for wood, ranging from commercial and institutional applications to multi-story residential developments in urban areas. While remaining deeply rooted in its craft tradition, wood is emerging as a building material with tremendous potential for innovation in the future.[7]

1 Kolb, Josef. *Systems in Timber Engineering.* Basel: Birkhäuser Verlag, 2008. 10–11.   **2** Schweitzer, Roland. "Wood as a Building Material – From the Beginnings to the 19th Century." *Timber Construction Manual.* By Thomas Herzog, Julius Natterer, Roland Schweitzer, Michael Volz, and Wolfgang Winter. Basel: Birkhäuser Verlag, 2004. 24–29.   **3** Mayo, Joseph. *Solid Wood.* New York: Routledge, 2015. 3–5.   **4** Kolb, Josef. 10–11.   **5** Dangel, Ulrich. *Sustainable Architecture in Vorarlberg: Energy Concepts and Construction Systems.* Basel: Birkhäuser Verlag, 2010. 62–63.   **6** Kaiser, Gabriele. "Von der Hand in den Kopf und im Blick das Ganze: Die Handwerkskultur der Familie K." *Zuschnitt: Zeitschrift über Holz als Werkstoff und Werke in Holz* 7.26 (2007). 10.   **7** Kolb, Josef. 10–11.

1

4

3

1 Japanese pagoda, Senso-ji temple, Tokyo
2 Church of the Transfiguration, Kizhi Pogost, Russia
3 North American tipi 4 Roof structure of a Mongolian
yurt 5 Traditional farmhouse, Austria

5

6

6 + 7 The development of modern construction systems in the late 20th century has revived the carpentry trade. Ölzbündt housing development, Dornbirn, Austria. Architect: Architekten Hermann Kaufmann ZT GmbH.   8 Digital fabrication   9 + 14 Modern lifting equipment   10 Prefabrication of components in the shop   11 + 12 Modular building systems   13 Modern transportation equipment

7

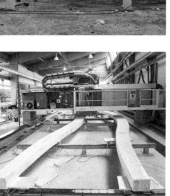

8

9

10

11

12

13

14

Timber Construction Systems

While historic styles of timber construction vary by region and culture, they have generally relied exclusively on linear structural members. Initially, these consisted of whole logs, but later construction techniques used beams, posts, and boards that were hewn by hand. The actual dimensions of trees and the members that could be cut from them limited structural spans and the overall size of buildings. Even though the invention of glued-laminated timber in the 19th century opened up possibilities of constructing larger structures with longer spans, it did not change the public perception that wood was primarily used for small-scale buildings. Over the last few decades, technological innovation and the development of new products have given rise to a number of structural systems that go beyond the limits of traditional wood construction. As a result, wood has become a viable alternative to steel and concrete for a range of building types from urban infill to mid- and high-rise structures. While linear structural members still form the basis of many of these new construction systems, the most innovative concepts employ additive strategies to create planar and spatial components that allow for an increasing degree of prefabrication.[1] The most prevalent historic techniques and contemporary systems are discussed below.

Log Construction

Log construction is a building technique in which timber members are stacked horizontally, one on top of another, and are interlocked in the corners using notched joints. Rigidity is achieved by these corner connections and by the frictional resistance developed between the members, rendering the need for mechanical fasteners unnecessary. The resulting solid-wood wall combines the functions of load-bearing structure, spatial enclosure, insulation, and exterior cladding in a single layer. Log buildings can be expected to settle, since the timber members are loaded perpendicularly to the grain, a dimension in which they are particularly susceptible to shrinkage. Therefore, the detailing of connections to other building materials and around openings should make allowance for considerable movement.[2]

Log construction is most common in areas where coniferous softwood trees are readily available to yield long, straight, structural members. These include the Alpine regions of Europe, the Scandinavian and Baltic states, the countries of Central Europe, and Russia. European immigrants brought this craft to North America, where other colonists and Native American tribes quickly adopted it. Log structures continue to be built today, with numerous variants emerging around the world, many times seemingly out of place. Thankfully, architects in regions with longstanding traditions of log construction have recognized their significance and are successfully reinterpreting vernacular building forms for contemporary yet contextual applications. Today, a single-layer log wall no longer satisfies the comfort and insulation requirements of contemporary standards of living. These increased demands have led to the development of more complex envelope assemblies consisting of several layers, each of which performs a specific function. The traditional handcrafted, hewn logs have mostly been replaced by a variety of sawn and milled log profiles that allow for a higher degree of prefabrication in the shop, while facilitating precise and quick assembly on site.[3]

Timber Frame Construction

Timber frame construction is a traditional method of building using heavy structural members that are squared-off in cross section. The individual components are carefully fitted together with traditional joinery techniques such as dovetail or mortise-and-tenon joints, which transfer loads in compression and are often secured with large wooden pegs (dowels), or nails. Diagonal members brace the framework laterally, while the infill panels have no structural function. Historically, the frame was usually filled in with wattle (a woven lattice of wooden sticks) and covered with daub (a combination of soil, clay, animal dung, straw, or other ingredients). Later building types adopted a masonry and plaster infill. The structural members typically remained exposed on the outside, but often they were subsequently covered up with plaster to resemble more expensive masonry buildings. The construction of these types of structures frequently took advantage of early forms of prefabrication, to the extent that the timbers were shaped and the joints fitted elsewhere, with the framework being finally assembled on site.[4]

Timber frame construction initially developed in climate zones that favored deciduous hardwood trees, which yielded relatively short structural members. This is the case in many countries of eastern and western Europe, with the most notable built examples located in Germany, Switzerland, Denmark, the Netherlands, France, and England. The earliest European settlers were also responsible for exporting the technique to North America. Japan's timber framing tradition stands out through its use of advanced joinery techniques that allow the creation of very rigid connections, therefore rendering diagonal bracing unnecessary. Heavy timber framing in its traditional form is no longer commonly employed for the construction of buildings today, but innovative engineered wood products and computer-controlled fabrication tools offer expanded opportunities for the development of new typologies based on its construction principles.[5]

Light Frame Construction

Fueled by rapid westward expansion and the need for buildings to be erected quickly, light frame construction was developed in the United States in the first half of the 19th century. Its proliferation was facilitated by the advent of the water-powered sawmill, which made boards and small wood framing members inexpensive and readily available, and by the industrial mass production of cheap nails. This led to the emergence of versatile building systems that allowed rapid construction with unskilled manual labor and a minimal use of tools. Easily handled by a single laborer, nominal 2-inch (5 cm) members of various depths are joined with only a few nails, while larger cross sections can be achieved simply by nailing several smaller sections together. Stud spacing of 16 or 24 inches (40 or 60 cm) on center is most common, and lateral stability of the framework is achieved by sheathing it with diagonal boards or wood panels, usually plywood or oriented strand board (OSB).

The earliest version of light framing was balloon frame construction, which utilizes studs that extend continuously over two stories from foundation to roof. Joists for intermediate floors are nailed to the studs, while a wood ribbon recessed into the studs provides additional support. Over time, the full-length studs proved to be too long for efficient erection, and the continuous cavities between studs facilitated the spread of fire to upper floors, unless they were closed off with a fire stop. Revisions were made to the system to address these issues, resulting in the development of several modified versions. Of these, platform frame construction emerged as the new universal standard. This system uses studs that are only one story high, regardless of the number of stories built. A floor platform is completed at each level, and the walls of the upper stories rest on platforms rather than directly on the walls of the story below. Even though standard details and framing practices are well established, the system remains easily and quickly adaptable in the field. In contrast to balloon framing, the lengths of framing lumber for walls are relatively short and easily handled. Due to the discontinuity of the wall studs, every story is automatically provided with a fire stop at each floor. The platform also serves as a convenient working surface for the carpenters building the frame, thus eliminating the need for scaffolding. The major disadvantage of the platform system is the fact that many wood members are loaded perpendicular to the grain, making the structure as a whole more susceptible to shrinkage. While the majority of framing members are made up of solid sawn lumber, the incorporation of engineered wood components (including I-joists, glulam beams, and veneer and strand lumber products) has increased over time. Due to its flexibility, speed of erection, and low cost, platform framing prevails as the most commonly used construction type for residential and small-scale commercial buildings in North America.[6]

Panel Construction
Inspired by North American light frame construction methods, early versions of panel construction systems were developed in Europe at the beginning of the 20th century, initially to provide cost-effective military shelters, and later to

address the housing shortage during and after the First World War.[7] The technique was reintroduced in the last quarter of the 20th century, triggering significant advancements in wood construction through its adaptation to European market conditions, levels of prefabrication, and high standards of quality and craftsmanship.

Similarly to platform framing, the structural system consists of a framework of load-bearing studs that is braced with sheathing. The degree of prefabrication is greater, however, with entire wall, floor, and roof panels being assembled in the shop and subsequently transported to the site for erection. Wall panels are typically one story tall, but element sizes are only limited by the constraints of transport, so assemblies can sometimes extend over several levels. Solid sawn lumber or glued-laminated lumber with a thickness of 60 mm (2⅜ in) is used for the studs, which are most commonly spaced at 62.5 cm (24 in) on center. The member depths match the thickness of the insulation that is inserted in between them, so panel thicknesses vary according to the particular insulation requirements. The sheathing consists of oriented strand board (OSB), gypsum board, fiberboard, or other engineered wood panel products.

Even though a defined set of rules is employed, panel construction remains an open building system that is customizable. Its widespread success is due to the fact that any qualified carpentry business can easily perform the necessary tasks without highly specialized equipment. Suitable for the construction of single-family residences, the technique has also grown in popularity with prefabricated housing manufacturers. A number of proprietary systems with high levels of prefabrication have been developed by the industry and are marketed for the construction of multi-story residential and commercial buildings. The increased use of computer-controlled materials handling and fabrication equipment ensures the quality and precision of the final product and facilitates smooth assembly on site.[8]

Frame Construction

Frame construction, also referred to as post-and-beam construction, evolved from traditional heavy timber framing methods. A structural framework of beams and columns carries the vertical loads, but it relies on a separate lateral bracing system, which can consist of shear walls, diagonal bracing, or a solid core. In order to achieve large spans and wide column spacing, the members are preferably made from glued-laminated timbers and other engineered wood products, but solid sawn timbers are also used. In most instances, individual components are joined by mechanical fasteners including bolts, lag screws, dowels, and concealed metal plate connectors.

Frame construction distinguishes itself from other timber construction systems by the fact that the system's load-bearing function is completely separated from that of spatial enclosure. This facilitates the incorporation of large expanses of glass into the facades and allows for highly flexible floor plan arrangements that can easily be adapted to changing user needs over time. Due to the separation of structure and enclosure, the load-bearing framework usually remains exposed. The rhythm and clarity of the structural system is therefore often instrumental in determining and enhancing a building's architectural character. While the envelope can be positioned inside or outside of the structure, or even in the same plane, containing the structural framework inside of a conditioned enclosure is preferred, since it avoids envelope penetrations, thermal bridges, and the exposure of timber elements to the weather.[9] The widespread proliferation of glued-laminated timber products since the 1960s has given timber frame construction an increased market share in areas that have traditionally been dominated by precast concrete systems. Today, its versatile applications include residential, commercial, and public buildings.[10]

Solid Timber Construction

Contemporary solid timber construction, also called mass timber construction, has emerged as an entirely new building system that has its origins in traditional log construction methods. Recent technological advancements have made it possible to combine individual wood members into load-bearing, large-format elements that exceed the structural limits of other common timber building components. These two-dimensional, planar units have the ability to resist both vertical and lateral forces, simultaneously providing the functions of load-bearing structure and spatial enclosure. They are employed for the construction of walls, floors, and roofs, and can even find application as staircase and elevator cores. Although solid timber elements perform well in the event of fire, they can be combined with steel and concrete into hybrid systems in situations where local fire code regulations are more restrictive and do not allow all-wood construction.[11]

Single-ply and multiple-ply panels most commonly consist of timber members that have been glued, doweled, or nailed together, yielding products that include cross-laminated timber (CLT), dowel-laminated timber (DLT), and nail-laminated timber (NLT). After the elements have been fabricated and the openings for doors and windows have been cut by computer-numerically controlled (CNC) machinery in the shop, they are usually transported to the construction site for final assembly. Higher degrees of prefabrication may include the off-site installation of windows, waterproofing, and exterior cladding. Most proprietary solid timber products on the market today feature solid cross sections, but there are also a number with compound cross sections that offer voids for the integration of building services and thermal or acoustic insulation. Providing that their interior surfaces are left exposed, solid timber elements have the advantage that their storage mass can be activated to improve thermal comfort. Additionally, moisture from the interior air can be absorbed and released, aiding in the regulation of interior humidity levels. In order to accommodate a variety of design solutions, solid timber panels can be combined with columns and beams made from glued-laminated timber or structural composite lumber products.[12]

As homogeneous structural products, solid timber components exhibit exceptional strength, making them suitable for the construction of tall buildings. Through the use of industrialized manufacturing methods, high levels of prefabrication, and rapid on-site assembly, solid timber construction systems are able to exploit the advantages of a modern factory set-up. This makes them increasingly cost effective, allowing them to provide comparable alternatives to more energy-intensive steel and concrete construction methods.[13]

1 Cheret, Peter, and Kurt Schwaner. "Holzbausysteme – eine Übersicht." *Handbuch und Planungshilfe Urbaner Holzbau.* Eds. Peter Cheret, Kurt Schwaner, and Arnim Seidel. Berlin: DOM Publishers, 2013. 114–29.   **2** Deplazes, Andrea. *Constructing Architecture: Materials, Processes, Structures.* Basel: Birkhäuser Verlag, 2005. 98.   **3** Kolb, Josef. *Systems in Timber Engineering.* Basel: Birkhäuser Verlag, 2008. 50–53.   **4** Deplazes, Andrea. 96.   **5** Kolb, Josef. 54–59.   **6** Allen, Edward, and Joseph Iano. *Fundamentals of Building Construction: Materials and Methods.* Hoboken, NJ: J. Wiley & Sons, 2004. 143–148.   **7** Winter, Stefan, and Frank Lattke. "Historische Entwicklung der Holzwand." *Zuschnitt: Zeitschrift über Holz als Werkstoff und Werke in Holz* 11.43 (2011). 14–15.   **8** Cheret, Peter, and Kurt Schwaner. 116–118; Kolb, Josef. 62–64.   **9** Kolb, Josef. 86–67, 108.   **10** Cheret, Peter, and Kurt Schwaner. 120–121.   **11** Mayo, Joseph. *Solid Wood.* New York: Routledge, 2015. 11–13.   **12** Kolb, Josef. 112–113.   **13** Smith, Ryan E., Gentry Griffin, and Talbot Rice. *Solid Timber Construction: Process, Practice, Performance.* Salt Lake City, UT: University of Utah, Integrated Technology in Architecture Center, College of Architecture and Planning, 2015. 5.

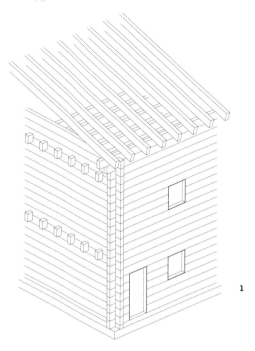

1

2

3

4

5

Log construction: **1** Construction   **2** Historic log
cabin, United States   **3** Contemporary log house under
construction: dovetail corner joint, Austria
4 Log house, Austria   **5** Locked lap joint, Austria

Timber frame construction: **6** Construction
7 Switzerland   **8** Germany   **9** Balloon frame construction   **10** Platform frame construction
11 Platform frame construction: single family
residence, United States

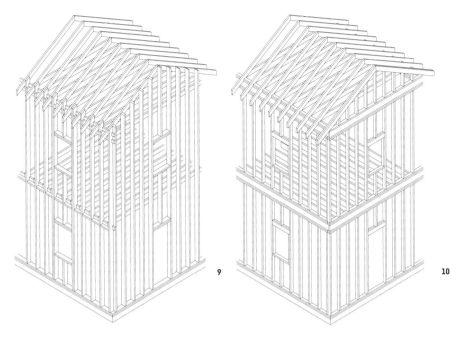

9

10

11

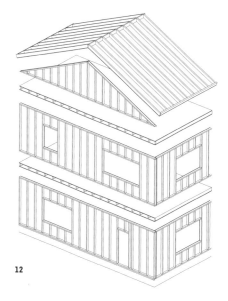

12

13

14

15

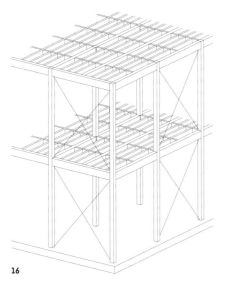

16

Panel construction: **12** Construction **13** Prefabrication in the shop **14** Insertion of insulation in the shop **15** Assembly on site **16 + 17** Frame construction **18** Frame construction. Tamedia Headquarters, Zurich. Architect: Shigeru Ban Architects. Engineer: Creation Holz GmbH.

17

18

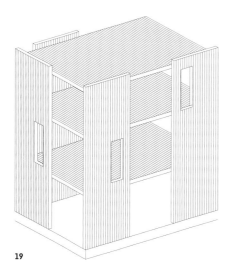

19

Solid timber construction: **19** Construction
20 Installation of cross-laminated timber wall and
floor panels on site   **21** Cross-laminated timber
wall panel with door and window cutouts made in the
shop   **22** Cross-laminated timber elevator cores

20

21

22

Wood-Based Composite Products

Wood-based composite products – also known as engineered wood products – have the potential to increase the value of forests as a resource by turning low-value raw materials into high-value commodities. They have largely been developed in response to the increased harvest of fast-growth, small-diameter trees that yield relatively low-grade wood. They combine the natural properties of wood with modern engineering and production technologies in the creation of resource-efficient products that can outperform solid-sawn lumber in many instances. Knots, inconsistencies, and other defects found in sawn lumber, which can affect strength and usability, are eliminated by binding together individual boards, veneers, strands, or fibers with adhesive or other fixing methods to form homogeneous large-format products. Shrinking and swelling due to changes in moisture are minimized, as are warping, splitting, twisting and other dimensional changes. The size of components that can be produced is only restricted by the limitations of the fabrication equipment and the constraints imposed by transportation. The manufacturers of wood-based composites are able to satisfy market requirements for strong, dimensionally stable products that are suitable for large spans, allowing them to compete structurally and economically with steel and concrete. While innovative wood-based composite products are continually being developed, the most commonly used types are described below.[1]

Glued-Laminated Timber (Glulam)

Glued-laminated timber is considered to be one of the oldest engineered wood products. The introduction of lamination technology at the end of the 19th century facilitated the production of structural timber members that were no longer constrained by the growth limits of trees.[2] Today, beams and columns of various sizes and shapes are produced by face-laminating three or more individual boards (known as "laminations") together. Prior to bonding, high-grade lumber boards are kiln-dried, stress-rated, sorted, and finger-jointed to form continuous laminations. These laminations are then pressed together using a system of adjustable and movable clamps, which permits the production of straight members, components with varying cross sections, arched and tapered shapes, as well as single and double-curved elements. Once the adhesive has cured, the timber members are planed, sanded, cut, and drilled as required for their particular use. Pressure treatment with preservatives is available for use in exterior applications. The manufacture of custom-laminated timber components is relatively labor-intensive and can be expensive, but standardized products are also available and can be mass-produced at lower costs.[3]

Structural Wood Panels

Over the last seventy-five years, structural panels have come to dominate the wood construction industry, and today plywood and oriented strand board (osb) constitute the two major types of products. Compared with conventional lumber, large-format panels offer greater speed of construction. They are predominantly used for roof and wall sheathing, subflooring, and shear bracing, but they also find application as concrete formwork, among other uses.[4]

Plywood consists of rotary-peeled veneers, known as "plies," which are glued together with phenolic resins so that the grain direction of each veneer layer is perpendicular to that of the adjacent layer. Assembling an odd number of layers ensures that the grain of the front and back faces runs in the same direction – which should be lengthwise along the panel – while the grain of one or more inner layers runs crosswise.[5] The technique of cross lamination provides plywood panels with excellent bending strength and stiffness properties along their two major axes as well as ensuring dimensional stability under changing moisture conditions.[6] While both softwoods and hardwoods are used for plywood production, the final species selection depends on the intended end use and the availability based on geographic location.

Oriented strand board is manufactured from thin wood strands that are generally 25 mm (1 in) wide, 150 mm (6 in) long, and less than 1 mm (1/32 in) thick. Arranged into loose mats of three to five layers, the strands in the outer faces are oriented lengthwise in the sheet, while the strands in the core are aligned crosswise or distributed randomly. Water-resistant phenol-formaldehyde or isocyanate adhesives are used to bond panels together under heat and pressure. The species used in osb production include low to medium-density woods such as aspen, pine, spruce, birch, poplar, and beech. The various layers of oriented strands provide osb with dimensional stability, as well as strength and stiffness characteristics that are very similar to those of plywood.[7] However, veneer logs for plywood manufacture are subject to stringent size and quality requirements and therefore represent a relatively high cost item. By employing lower-grade, faster-growing species, osb can be produced at a lower cost while making more efficient use of forest resources. These distinct advantages have led to osb superseding plywood for many construction applications throughout the industry, significantly increasing its market share. Besides its utilization as roof, wall, and floor sheathing, osb also commonly serves as the web of prefabricated I-joists and the skin of structural insulated panels (sips).[8]

Laminated Veneer Lumber (LVL)

Laminated veneer lumber consists of rotary-peeled veneers that are bonded together under heat and pressure into large billets, which are subsequently cut
into a variety of widths depending on their end-use application. A continuous
production process allows the creation of member sizes that go beyond conventional lumber lengths. The wood species commonly used include pine, spruce,
Douglas fir, larch, and poplar, while phenol-formaldehyde resins provide waterproof bonds. Defects are evenly distributed throughout the material, resulting in
enhanced strength properties and dimensional stability when compared with
solid-sawn lumber.[9] With veneer thicknesses ranging from 1.5 to 6 mm (0.06
to 0.25 in), the grain of all plies generally runs lengthwise, making members
produced in this fashion suitable for use as beams, trusses, planks, and rafters. However, LVL can also be manufactured with some veneers oriented at 90
degrees to the main axis. This cross-bonded structure provides increased stiffness and shear resistance as well as allowing the manufacture of wall and floor
panels with both load-bearing and bracing capacity. LVL members can easily be
treated with preservatives for use in situations where they are prone to insect
or fungi attack.[10]

Parallel Strand Lumber (PSL)

Parallel strand lumber is produced from long strands of veneer that are laid lengthwise in parallel and glued together in a continuous press. The veneer strips are
about 3 mm (⅛ in) thick, 19 mm (¾ in) wide, and at least 60 cm (24 in) long.
PSL manufacture, currently limited to North America, can utilize waste material from plywood and LVL production, and the species commonly used include
Douglas fir, southern pine, western hemlock, and yellow poplar. Individual
strands are bonded together to form members up to 20 m (66 ft) long, using
waterproof adhesives with a phenol-formaldehyde base, which are cured using
microwave technology.[11] The relatively large proportion of small voids in the
finished product enables a high degree of preservative penetration, allowing its
use in severe exterior conditions. Due to its high bending strength, PSL is commonly used for large headers, long-span beams, and heavily loaded columns,
while its appealing appearance makes it suitable for exposed applications.[12]

Laminated Strand Lumber (LSL)

Laminated strand lumber is similar to parallel strand lumber, but it consists of
flaked wood strands that are roughly 1 mm (¹⁄₃₂ in) thick, 25 mm (1 in) wide, and
30 cm (12 in) long.[13] Its manufacture uses small-diameter trees of fast-growing species such as aspen, poplar, basswood, and other low-density hardwoods,
which are generally not suitable for the production of conventional solid-sawn
lumber. The strands are commonly blended with waterproof isocyanate adhe-

sives, arranged into loose mats parallel to the longitudinal axis of the member, and cured in steam injection presses.[14] The cured billets are cut into a range of member sizes that are suitable for use as beams, rafters, headers, sill plates, and studs. LSL products exhibit good weatherability and dimensional stability, and they resemble oriented strand board in appearance since they are made from the same raw material.[15]

Cross-Laminated Timber (CLT)

Initially developed in Europe in the 1990s, cross-laminated timber consists of several layers of lumber board that are stacked at right angles to one another and glued face-to-face to form large-format structural panels. Individual boards are finger-jointed to achieve the required member lengths and are sometimes edge-glued as well. To ensure symmetry in cross section, CLT products are fabricated with an odd number of layers – three to seven being the most common – but more layers are also possible. The grain of the outer layers always runs parallel to the principal load direction of the panel. While adjacent layers are typically arranged at right angles to one another, they may be arranged parallel so as to obtain panel products with increased load-bearing capacities.[16] CLT manufacture uses a variety of softwood species including spruce, fir, pine, and larch, which are commonly bonded using formaldehyde-free, one-component polyurethane (PUR) or emulsion polymer isocyanate (EPI) adhesives.[17] The glued-up panels are pressed in hydraulic presses or vacuum presses, cured, sanded, and cut to size. Openings for doors, windows, stairs, and mechanical services can be pre-cut in the factory using computer-numerically controlled (CNC) machinery. While maximum sizes vary by manufacturer, panels are typically manufactured up to 2.95 m (10 ft) wide, 16 m (52 ft) long, and up to 300 mm (12 in) thick.[18] Panels with larger dimensions are possible, but these may be limited by transportation and assembly restrictions. The cross-lamination of panels yields exceptionally strong and dimensionally stable products with bi-directional load-bearing capacity, which are particularly suitable for use as floors, walls, and roofs in multi-story applications.

Nailed and Doweled Solid Timber

Mechanical connections can be used instead of adhesives, notably in the production of solid timber elements. The use of chemical compounds that might emit potentially harmful substances can be avoided in this way, which is an advantage in terms of indoor air quality. Mechanical fasteners also help to resolve issues of reuse, recycling, or disposal once a wood product reaches the end of its service life.[19]

Nail-laminated timber (NLT) is created from softwood lumber boards stacked on edge and fastened together with nails to form dimensionally stable panels. Individual pieces are sometimes finger-jointed to enable the fabrication of larger formats. Plywood or OSB sheathing is often added to one side of the panel to create a structural diaphragm. NLT floor systems have been in use for more than a century, in particular in heavy timber industrial buildings where they were combined with solid-sawn timber post-and-beam construction. Today, nail-laminated timber is most commonly used for floor, wall, and roof applications, but it may also be employed for elevator and staircase shafts.[20] Its simplicity and ease of fabrication allows most qualified timber manufacturers to produce these types of prefabricated elements. Individual boards are usually 20 to 50 mm (¾ to 2 in) thick, with panel thicknesses ranging from 80 to 240 mm (3 to 9 in).[21]

Dowel-laminated timber (DLT) is similar in configuration, but it uses dowels of wood or metal to bind laminations together. The use of wood dowels enables the creation of products that are entirely made from timber, thus greatly facilitating end-of-life material recovery and repurposing. In this process, softwood boards with a moisture content of 12 to 15 percent are fastened together with hardwood dowels, often made from beech, that possess a lower moisture content of around 8 percent. As the wooden dowels absorb moisture, they expand and effectively lock the individual planks tightly together.[22] Dowel-laminated timber can also be fabricated using a cross-banded arrangement of layers. By orienting boards vertically, horizontally, and diagonally to each other, these types of elements share many similarities with CLT panels and are most often used for wall applications. Wood fiber insulation boards can easily be incorporated into the panel buildup, rounding off the all-wood product concept.[23]

Another solid timber product relying on mechanical connections is interlocking cross-laminated timber (ICLT), which uses dovetail joints to bond individual laminations together.[24] Unlike other solid wood panel products, ICLT uses no adhesives or fasteners, but instead relies on traditional wood joinery techniques, simplifying the disassembly of panels at the end of their lives.

Adhesives

The manufacture of most engineered wood products relies on adhesives, which transfer and distribute loads between individual components such as veneers, strands, and fibers. They provide strength and stiffness immediately after manufacture and must continue to perform reliably for long-term use. For centuries, natural polymer adhesives derived from plants and animals were used for bonding wood. Made from blood, animal hide, casein, soybean, starch, dextrin, and other biomass, many are still in use today, but fossil fuel-based products have mostly replaced them. These synthetic adhesives, introduced in the 1930s, are able to provide modern engineered wood products with the necessary strength, durability, and water resistance. Recent technological developments have resulted, however, in significant improvements in the manufacture of biomass-based glues, and their market share is expected to increase in the future.[25]

Selecting the right adhesive from the many different types available today depends on many factors, including strength requirements, application method, fire performance, bonding characteristics, curing needs, and cost. Among the adhesives for interior, non-structural applications are urea formaldehyde, hot melt glue, and natural polymers. Due to their low heat and moisture-resistance, they are mostly used in products such as particleboard and medium density fiberboard (MDF) for fabricating furniture, cabinetry, and architectural millwork. The most common synthetic wood resins for structural applications include phenol-formaldehyde (PF), resorcinol-formaldehyde (RF), phenol-resorcinol-formaldehyde (PRF), melamine-formaldehyde (MF), melamine-urea-formaldehyde (MUF), polyurethane (PUR), polymeric methylene diphenyl diisocyanate (PMDI), and emulsion polymer isocyanate (EPI).[26] These adhesives, which are generally water-resistant as well as stronger and stiffer than the actual wood they bond, have gained wide acceptance for the manufacture of wood-based composite products.

Health and safety concerns over the use of wood adhesives arose in the 1980s, when formaldehyde, a hardener contained in many adhesives, was identified as a severe irritant and probable carcinogen.[27] As a result, numerous countries imposed regulations to lower formaldehyde emissions, which led to the formulation of stricter emission limits for both manufacturing processes and finished wood products. Many resins such as phenol-(resorcinol)-formaldehyde and melamine-formaldehyde polymers are highly stable and do not off-gas once bonded. Products made with urea-formaldehyde adhesives, in contrast, can release low concentrations of formaldehyde even when cured.[28] To address the ongoing concern over off-gassing, several types of ultra-low emitting formaldehyde (ULEF) resin have been developed. Depending on the application, isocyanate (PMDI and EPI), polyvinyl acetate (PVA), and soy adhesives can also serve as suitable alternatives, since they are no-added formaldehyde (NAF) products.[29]

1 Bowyer, Jim L., Rubin Shmulsky, and John G. Haygreen. *Forest Products and Wood Science: An Introduction.* 5th ed. Ames, IA: Blackwell, 2007. 353, 415. **2** Steurer, Anton. *Developments in Timber Engineering: The Swiss Contribution.* Basel: Birkhäuser Verlag, 2006. 74. **3** Bowyer, Jim L., Rubin Shmulsky, and John G. Haygreen. 416–420. **4** Bowyer, Jim L., Rubin Shmulsky, and John G. Haygreen. 353–354. **5** Allen, Edward, and Joseph Iano. *Fundamentals of Building Construction: Materials and Methods.* Hoboken, NJ: J. Wiley & Sons, 2004. 95. **6** "Plywood." Panel Products. Canadian Wood Council. Web. 21 Jan. 2016. **7** Stark, Nicole M., Zhiyong Cai, and Charles Carll. "Wood-Based Composite Materials." *Wood Handbook: Wood as an Engineering Material.* Madison, WI: United States Department of Agriculture, Forest Service, Forest Products Laboratory, 2010. 11–7/8.

8 "OSB." *Panel Products.* Canadian Wood Council. Web. 21 Jan. 2016. **9** Bowyer, Jim L., Rubin Shmulsky, and John G. Haygreen. 420–423. **10** "Furnierschichtholz." *Dataholz.com.* Holzforschung Austria, Jan. 2013. Web. 18 Jan. 2016. **11** Stark, Nicole M., Zhiyong Cai, and Charles Carll. 11–21. **12** "Parallel Strand Lumber." *Structural Composite.* Canadian Wood Council, Web. 19 Jan. 2016. **13** "Spanstreifenholz." *Dataholz.com.* Holzforschung Austria, Jan. 2013. Web. 19 Jan. 2016. **14** Bowyer, Jim L., Rubin Shmulsky, and John G. Haygreen. 423–427. **15** "Laminated Strand Lumber." *Structural Composite.* Canadian Wood Council, Web. 19 Jan. 2016. **16** Gagnon, Sylvain, E.M. (Ted) Bilek, Lisa Podesto, and Pablo Crespell. "Introduction to Cross-Laminated Timber." *CLT Handbook: Cross-Laminated Timber.* Eds. Erol Karacabeyli and Brad Douglas. Pointe-Claire, QC: FPInnovations, Binational Softwood Lumber Council, 2013. 3. **17** Yeh, Borjen, Dave Kretschmann, and Brad (Jianhe) Wang. "Cross-Laminated Timber Manufacturing." *CLT Handbook: Cross-Laminated Timber.* Eds. Erol Karacabeyli and Brad Douglas. Pointe-Claire, QC: FPInnovations, Binational Softwood Lumber Council, 2013. 3–4. **18** *Bauen mit Brettsperrholz: Holzbau Handbuch,* Reihe 4, Teil 6, Folge 1. Berlin: Informationsdienst Holz, 2012. 8. **19** Mayo, Joseph. *Solid Wood.* New York: Routledge, 2015. 17. **20** "Nail Laminated Timber (NLT)." *Nail Laminated Timber (NLT).* ReThink Wood. 28 Jan. 2016. **21** Kolb, Josef. *Systems in Timber Engineering.* Basel: Birkhäuser Verlag, 2008. 122. **22** Mayo, Joseph. 18. **23** Kolb, Josef. 124. **24** Gagnon, Sylvain, E.M. (Ted) Bilek, Lisa Podesto, and Pablo Crespell. 3. **25** Frihart, Charles R., and Christopher G. Hunt. "Adhesives with Wood Materials: Bond Formation and Performance." *Wood Handbook: Wood as an Engineering Material.* Madison, WI: United States Department of Agriculture, Forest Service, Forest Products Laboratory, 2010. 10–8. **26** *Adhesives Awareness Guide.* Leesburg, VA: American Wood Council. 2. **27** Bowyer, Jim L., Rubin Shmulsky, and John G. Haygreen. 392. **28** Frihart, Charles R., and Christopher G. Hunt. 10–14. **29** "No-Added Formaldehyde (NAF) and Ultra Low Emitting Formaldehyde Resins (ULEF)." *Composite Wood Products ATCM.* California Environmental Protection Agency, Air Resources Board, 24 Dec. 2015. Web. 1 Feb. 2016.

1 Glued-laminated timber (glulam) **2** Laminated veneer lumber (LVL) **3** Oriented strand board (OSB) **4** Plywood **5** Parallel strand lumber (PSL) **6** Laminated strand lumber (LSL)

7

7 Cross-laminated timber (CLT)   **8** Nail-laminated
timber (NLT) panels   **9 + 10** Dowel-laminated timber
(DLT), front and side view   **11 + 12** Glulam production   **13** Application of adhesive   **14** CLT production

8

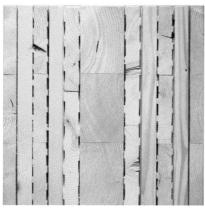

9

10

11

12

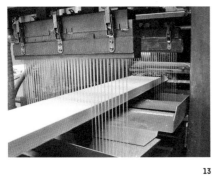

13

14

Hybrid Construction and Composite Components

Most buildings today are erected using hybrid construction techniques that utilize a combination of different materials for technical, functional, or aesthetic reasons. This allows the strengths of a particular construction material to be exploited while its weaknesses are compensated for by another, leading to optimization of the structure as a whole.[1] When building with wood, non-combustible elements made of steel or concrete are frequently incorporated to enhance characteristics such as structural capacity, fire resistance, and acoustic performance, often in response to local building code requirements. While it is theoretically possible to construct a building completely out of wood, even a "pure" timber structure usually relies on metal parts. Contemporary wood construction is barely viable without the use of nails, screws, bolts, and plates for common connections between building components. Wood elements loaded in compression are often combined with structural steel members that act in tension, thus forming hybrid beams and columns. Taking advantage of each material's intrinsic strength allows longer spans with increased spatial flexibility, as well as a reduction in structural mass that is often accompanied by a certain lightness of appearance. Concrete construction is generally employed for the podium level of multi-story timber buildings to ensure that the load-bearing wood structure is adequately protected from moisture, insect infestation, and damage from vehicular impact. Also, using concrete walls for cores, staircases, and elevator shafts is an effective means of fireproofing circulation spaces while providing lateral load resistance for the entire building.

Post-tensioned timber systems unite the high tensile strength of steel with the benefits of glued-laminated timber, laminated veneer lumber, or cross-laminated timber products. The beams, columns, and panels are manufactured with continuous internal ducts into which steel tendons are inserted. Once the building frame has been assembled, the tendons are tensioned, generating a rigid structure with moment-resisting connections. With their reduced mass and resulting low embodied energy levels, these systems provide good lateral load-resistance; they are therefore well suited for multi-story applications in seismically active zones or regions with high wind loads.[2] Composite technology enables the bonding of carbon, fiberglass, or aramid fibers to glued-laminated timber. These high-strength synthetic fibers are integrated into the tensile zones of beams using various types of resin, yielding exceptionally strong and stiff fiber-reinforced timber members with higher load-bearing capacities but smaller cross sections than conventional glulam beams. This method even allows pre-tensioning, which further improves the structural performance of members subjected to high bending stresses.[3]

Wood-concrete composite construction is mainly used for floor systems, which in such cases consist of a concrete slab that is integrally connected to timber beams or a laminated timber panel. Their combined structural performance is optimized through the creation of composite action between the two materials. The concrete resists in compression while the wood develops tensile resistance, thus taking advantage of each material's structural attributes. Increased stiffness and strength allow longer spans and higher load-bearing capacities, while the system itself possesses a relatively low dead load compared with all-concrete or all-steel construction. The concrete topping slab adds thermal mass, improves fire resistance, and enhances impact and airborne sound insulation, while the timber structure serves as permanent formwork and provides an aesthetically pleasing ceiling surface.[4] A number of different wood products can be used for composite floor systems, ranging from solid timber and glulam beams to cross-laminated timber, nail-laminated timber, and dowel-laminated timber panels. Critical for the creation of composite action is the shear connection between the wood and concrete, which can be achieved through the use of metal fasteners or by interlocking the two materials. The shear connectors used include anchor bolts, steel dowels, proprietary diagonally inserted screws, and expanded metal mesh strips that are bonded into grooves routed into the wood. Alternatively, the wood surface can receive notches or be profiled to allow the transfer of shear forces. In the on-site casting process, first the prefabricated timber elements are installed, then the reinforcement and shear connectors are placed, and finally the concrete slab is poured. This has the advantage of creating a continuous diaphragm that aids in the distribution of lateral loads.

It is also possible to prefabricate composite floors completely off-site in a shop environment, which can speed up construction, but the joints between the precast panels still need to be reinforced and filled through on-site casting.[5] New developments include the separate shop fabrication of the timber structure and the precast concrete slabs for subsequent connection on site. The two elements are joined with long screws, which are inserted through angled sleeves that have been cast into the concrete panels. This ensures composite action while greatly facilitating the separation of materials at the end of the building's life. Research is currently under way into the use of adhesive strips to establish an easily reversible connection between wood and concrete.[6] Wood-concrete composite systems today are extremely customizable and allow varying degrees of prefabrication. Their versatility makes them suitable for a wide range of applications including floors and walls for new buildings, the restoration of existing buildings, and timber bridge construction.[7]

Wood is valued for its many beneficial characteristics, including lower embodied energy levels, recyclability, and renewability. These environmental advantages are jeopardized when wood is combined with less sustainable materials. When considering wood composite construction, it is therefore imperative to address issues of assembly and disassembly carefully, as well as reusability and recyclability.

1 *Holzkonstruktionen in Mischbauweise: Holzbau Handbuch,* Reihe 1, Teil 1, Folge 5. Bonn: Holzabsatzfonds, 2006. 19.   2 Mayo, Joseph. *Solid Wood.* New York: Routledge, 2015. 19–20.   3 Trummer, Andreas, and Wilhelm F. Luggin. "Holz | Hochfeste Fasern: Leistungssteigerung durch Bewehrung." *Zuschnitt: Zeitschrift über Holz als Werkstoff und Werke in Holz* 5.17 (2005). 24.   4 *Holzkonstruktionen in Mischbauweise: Holzbau Handbuch.* 46–51.   5 Kolb, Josef. *Systems in Timber Engineering.* Basel: Birkhäuser Verlag, 2008. 180–181.   6 "Mit pragmatischen Überlegungen die richtige Konstruktion finden – ein Gespräch mit Hermann Kaufmann." *Detail: Zeitschrift für Architektur und Baudetail* 12.2015 (2015). 1232–1237.   7 *Holzkonstruktionen in Mischbauweise: Holzbau Handbuch.* 46–51.

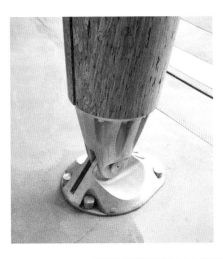

1 Cast steel column footing **2** Steel plate connectors **3** Hybrid truss with steel tension members. Arena, Université du Québec à Chicoutimi, Québec. Architect: lemay montréal, Les Architectes Associés Boulay – Fradette – Boudreault. Engineer: Nordic Structures, Groupe Stavibel.

4

5

6

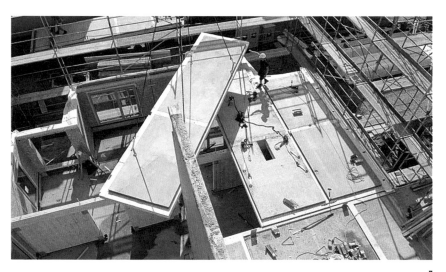

7

8

9

4 Post-tensioned timber structure undergoing shaking table test at the University of Basilicata, Potenza, Italy   **5** Post-tensioned timber structure: anchorage of steel tendons. ETH House of Natural Resources, Zurich.   **6** Concrete podium   **7** Wood-concrete composite slab   **8** Wood-concrete composite construction: insertion of expanded metal mesh shear connectors   **9** Wood-concrete composite system: timber structure and precast concrete slabs are fabricated separately and connected with diagonally inserted screws on site, facilitating separation of materials at the end of the building's life.   **10** Wood-concrete composite slab

10

Prefabrication and Mass Customization

Contemporary timber construction takes advantage of wood's many beneficial characteristics; among these are its lightness and ease of workability, which make
it particularly suitable for prefabrication. Throughout history, carpenters have
endeavored to prefabricate as many components and connections as possible
before erecting a structure. The tradition of trimming, fitting, and joining members in the shop or on the construction site can be considered one of the earliest
forms of prefabrication. Prefabricated timber construction offers alternatives to
conventional building practices, which are often plagued by inclement weather,
exceeding budgets, chronic delays, and poor quality of construction.[1]

Prefabrication allows construction processes to be undertaken simultaneously
rather than in a linear fashion, thus leading to a reduction of on-site erection
work and overall construction time. Site preparation and foundation work, for
instance, can be completed while structural components are being manufactured in the shop. Fabrication in a protected facility eliminates the impact of
weather disruption and ensures on-time delivery. Earlier project completion
and occupancy can bring a quicker return on investment. A dry and safe working environment contributes to improved conditions for personnel while reducing the risk of jobsite injuries. The use of jigs and handling equipment for the
assembly of wall, ceiling, and floor elements ensures consistency and precision,
and facilitates quality assurance. Since prefabricated elements can be promptly
installed once delivered to the site, the potential for damage to finished products is also greatly reduced. One of the environmental benefits of shop fabrication is the more efficient use of material and the significant decrease in on-site
waste, reducing the amount of material to be disposed of as landfill. Lastly, the
rapid installation of components on site minimizes noise pollution and the disruption of day-to-day operations for adjacent neighbors, particularly in dense
urban areas.[2]

Levels of prefabrication vary depending on the intended application and their
practical feasibility. Prefabricated components often come in the form of solid-
sawn or laminated timber beams and columns, which are cut to size and fitted
to receive a variety of connectors for final assembly on site. Prefabricated panels involve the manufacture of large-format wall or floor elements in the shop,
which are then flat-packed and shipped to the site. Both load-bearing and non-
load-bearing panels are possible; these may be delivered with insulation, air
barriers, vapor retarders, windows, doors, interior finishes, and exterior cladding installed.[3] Lastly, entire prefabricated modules may be assembled at an off-
site location to include interior and exterior finishes, mechanical, electrical, and
plumbing services and fixtures, and sometimes even furnishings. Since most
of them are shipped by truck, their overall dimensions are usually limited by
the locally applicable road transport regulations. Modules typically arrive at the

jobsite 80 to 95 percent complete, are self-supporting, and are stacked on top of one another by crane. They are particularly well suited to building types that do not require large, open spans and have a high degree of repetition, such as multi-family housing, hotels, dormitories, and nursing homes.[4] Contemporary frame construction often employs a combination of prefabricated structural components and panels, while the techniques of panel construction and solid timber construction both make use of prefabricated panels and modules.[5]

While high degrees of prefabrication usually involve elevated labor and material costs in the shop, savings can be realized through efficient delivery logistics, sequencing, and pre-installing elements that considerably decrease on-site construction time. Maximizing the dimensions of components, panels, and modules minimizes the number of joints, which are susceptible to air and water infiltration, and reduces the number of connections that have to be made in the field. The expense of transportation can be substantial and needs to be considered, but it is often balanced out by avoiding costly and prolonged work on site. Since it is not easy to modify prefabricated elements in the field, an intensive and detailed planning phase is required to ensure proper coordination between all of the trades involved. This can also improve cost transparency.[6]

Many early prefabrication concepts were based on systems consisting of highly uniform parts with standardized dimensions, which could be combined in various configurations to satisfy a multitude of applications. Although this allowed cost-efficient construction through the mass production of components, it more often than not denied buildings an identity of their own. The development of sophisticated, computer-controlled fabrication equipment over the last thirty years has increased the range of opportunities for customized solutions. While a systematic and integrated approach is still usual, modern prefabrication is focused less on the uniformity of parts than on dividing designs into manageable units that can easily be handled and transported. This avoids a relentlessly monotonous appearance and allows buildings to be highly tailored while taking advantage of the efficiencies of prefabrication. The major downside is that buildings conceived in this manner still remain one-of-a-kind prototypes in most cases. The process of mass customization, which is commonly used in the manufacture of many consumer products today, can offer an outstanding solution for this issue. A comprehensive system based on this concept provides standardized core components, connections, and assemblies that ensure economy, consistency, and quality control, but it also allows for modifications to achieve custom-tailored buildings that meet diverse and changing client needs. Although they require close collaboration between architects, engineers, and fabricators, these new types of open timber building systems can readily be adapted for a range of building types in the future.[7]

1 Kaufmann, Hermann. "The 'Other' Building Process." *Building with Timber: Paths into the Future*. Eds. Hermann Kaufmann and Winfried Nerdinger. Munich: Prestel, 2011. 42.   **2** *Putting the Pieces Together. WW-016*. Wood-Works, 2014.   **3** Mayo, Joseph. *Solid Wood*. New York: Routledge, 2015. 24.   **4** *Putting the Pieces Together*. **5** "Die Logik der Vorfertigung: Eine Systemübersicht." *Zeitschrift über Holz als Werkstoff und Werke in Holz* 13.50 (2013). 12–13.   **6** Mayo, Joseph. 24.   **7** Kaufmann, Hermann. 45.

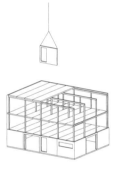  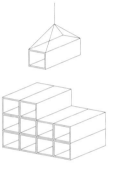

Prefabricated Components
and Panels

Prefabricated Panels

Prefabricated Modules

1 Carpenters shaping a beam. Austria, 1906.
2 Levels of prefabrication

3

4

5

6

3 Prefabricated components: glued-laminated timber beams   **4** Prefabricated components: I-joists
5 Prefabrication of panels in the shop   **6** Prefabrication of modules in the shop   **7** Prefabricated panel
8 Prefabricated modules   **9** The LifeCycle Tower One (LCT One) is a prototype structure that was built using an open timber building system, which can be adapted to a variety of building typologies. Dornbirn, Austria. Architect: Architekten Hermann Kaufmann ZT GmbH. Engineer: merz kley partner. Client: CREE GmbH.

7

8

9

Wood Technology and Digital Manufacturing

The carpenter traditionally united the roles of the contemporary architect, structural engineer, and fabricator in one person. He was in charge of developing a comprehensive design, sizing the structure, and manufacturing the individual parts: a process that concluded with the assembly of all of the components on site. After essential design features had been agreed upon with the client, the carpenter followed customary rules of practice for selecting the type of construction, determining the building's geometry, and developing the details. Taking into account the material's natural characteristics, his work was defined by concerns for overall composition and proportions rather than precise measurements. While every building was shaped using the same principles, this approach brought forth highly individual design solutions, resulting in no two structures being exactly alike.[1] The carpenter's responsibilities included logging the timber and shaping the logs into usable wood for construction. These tasks were performed with manual tools, which remained virtually unchanged between the Middle Ages and the 19th century. The Industrial Revolution led to the introduction of machinery, which facilitated the mass production of solid-sawn lumber in standard sizes that could easily be transported and sold to distant markets. New processing techniques also emerged, allowing the development of improved composite products such as glued-laminated timber beams and plywood panels, which effectively eliminated the anisotropic characteristics of wood. Traditional joinery techniques that had been established over hundreds of years were increasingly superseded by the use of mass-produced, standardized fasteners including nails and screws. Growing specialization in the construction industry meant that carpenters had to relinquish many of their responsibilities to the newly established professions of architect and engineer, who took over design and planning processes.[2]

Computer-numerically controlled (CNC) machines, which first appeared in the 1980s, have dramatically transformed the wood-manufacturing trade. Unlike conventional equipment, which only allows the serial production of standardized commodities, digitally controlled equipment offers the ability to fabricate highly customized components of varying shape and size without any notable loss of productivity. Called "computer-aided manufacturing" (CAM), this process employs computer-aided design (CAD) software to generate two- and three-dimensional forms, which can then be translated to the fabrication software used to control the tool. The most common equipment are joinery machines for linear members, which can complete numerous tasks including cutting, planing, drilling, milling, and joining. The more recently developed gantry machining centers expand these capabilities to process large-format panel products such as cross-laminated timber elements. Integrated automatic tool changers streamline the workflow by enabling the machines to select from a multitude of different tool heads.[3] CNC machines with three degrees of freedom can move and cut along the X, Y, and Z axes, but they make cutting at an angle extremely difficult or tedious. Five-axis machines, on the other hand, feature a tool head that can rotate about two additional axes and thereby offer increased functionality for manufacturing.[4] Complex and curved geometries can easily be achieved, while the use of digital processes ensures high levels of precision during fabrication and minimizes tolerances for later erection on site. The development of early CAM machines mostly led to an automatization of manual techniques previously performed by carpenters, but the latest generation of equipment consists of extremely versatile robots with six or more degrees of freedom that enable entirely new types of operations.[5] These tools are supported by advanced digital form-finding processes that include parametric and algorithmic modeling procedures. Frequently, however, these design methods do not take wood's distinct properties into account, with the result that they impose elaborate geometries and devise thousands of differently sized and shaped components. This can increase the effort of assembly on site considerably – a task that is essentially still performed by humans.

Today, efficient digital processes have significantly streamlined day-to-day operations in the wood manufacturing industry. They facilitate collaboration and communication between the designer, the engineer, and the fabricator, they simplify the production of customized prefabricated building components, and they coordinate logistics for transport and assembly. The use of comprehensive 3D models is expected to optimize construction practices further. Generated with building information modeling (BIM) software, these models will contain all of the essential physical and functional characteristics of a project over its entire life cycle, from design and fabrication to assembly and disassembly. Current research projects at universities and institutions around the world suggest that digital design and fabrication methods will continue to advance and to increase in complexity. The utmost care and reason should be employed to ensure that the unique characteristics of wood and its ecological potential are not compromised by the fascination with new geometries that are being made possible and rationalized by the latest technological achievements. Going beyond purely formal explorations, informed computer-based design and fabrication processes have significant potential to resolve issues of material use, waste minimization, structural efficiency, and form, ultimately leading to an overall optimization of timber construction systems.

1 Buri, Hani, and Yves Weinand. "The Tectonics of Timber Architecture in the Digital Age." *Building with Timber: Paths into the Future*. Eds. Hermann Kaufmann and Winfried Nerdinger. Prestel: Munich, 2010. 56–63. **2** Sagmeister, Rudolf, and Kathleen Sagmeister. *Holzbaukunst in Vorarlberg*. Bregenz: Eugen-Ruß-Verlag, 1988. 7–15.   **3** "Glossar Digitaler Holzbau." *Zuschnitt: Zeitschrift über Holz als Werkstoff und Werke in Holz* 14.53 [2014]. 24.   **4** Buri, Hani, and Yves Weinand. 56–63.   **5** "Die Grenzen der Geschicklichkeit." *Holzbau Austria*. Holzbau Austria – Fachmagazin für Holzbau und Nachhaltige Architektur. Web. 24 Feb. 2016.

1 The most important tools of the carpentry trade:
double-bitted mortising ax, broad ax, frame saw,
and goniometer   2 Industrial band saw cutting a log
into boards   3 Joinery machine   4 Gantry machining
center   5 Automatic tool changer

6

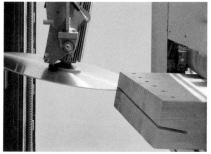

7

8

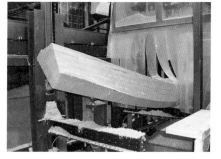

9

10

11

6 Slanted drilling   **7** Slot cutting   **8** Portal robot
9 Milling of complex geometries   **10** Milling
11 Planing   **12** New technologies enable complex
geometries

12

Craft Tradition and Future

Craft accompanied mankind from its early days and flourished long before the trades formally organized themselves into guilds during the Middle Ages. Materials were shaped into weapons, household items, and structures for shelter – initially by hand, but later increasingly through the use of tools.[1] Wood is presumably the second-oldest material to have been worked by the human hand, after stone, which positions it at the very beginning of the history of craft. The knowledge and skills of woodworking were amassed and handed down over thousands of years, aiding in the development of a craft tradition and culture that became integral to timber construction.[2]

Craftsmanship can be described as springing from a basic human desire to perform a task well for its own sake. It unites the development of a theoretical notion and its implementation as a physical object in one activity, thus involving its author in a continuous dialog between conceptual thinking and tangible practice. The mind controls the hand, while the actions of hand and tool simultaneously feed back into the thinking process. Craftsmanship necessitates patience, determination, and perseverance, and it is founded on the repetition and perfection of skills to a high degree over thousands of hours. Once a technique has been mastered, it is no longer a merely mechanical activity, but part of the craftsperson's expertise, allowing more holistic thinking and working.[3] Craft requires intimate knowledge of a material's characteristics since they shape both the process and the final product. The experienced craftsperson employs his or her skills to work with a material and its unique qualities in order to achieve excellence.[4]

Throughout history, society has repeatedly devalued the practical aspects of craft and has isolated it from higher intellectual pursuits.[5] It is craft's holistic approach, however, that distinguishes it from industrial practices. The Industrial Revolution in the 19th century fragmented work processes into numerous individual operations, each of which could easily and consistently be repeated by semi-skilled labor. This was essential to the mass production of identical goods destined for a large consumer base. In contrast, craft requires its author to be fully engaged in the entire process from the procurement of raw materials and the design development to the manufacture and final delivery of the completed work. The craftsperson's commitment, expertise, and experience yield one-of-a-kind artifacts.[6] Nevertheless, at the time, craftsmanship was considered starkly juxtaposed to the imperatives and promises of technological advancement and the associated modern lifestyle. After industrialization, the digital revolution at the end of the 20th century caused a second major identity crisis for craft, when the automation of design and manufacturing processes began to apply further pressure on the validity of traditional knowledge and skills. In recent years, the ubiquitous presence of mass-produced, interchangeable consumer goods in an increasingly globalized world has raised the demand for skillfully crafted products made locally, satisfying the general public's longing for more conscious consumption. Craftsmanship is once again appreciated for its unique qualities, while establishing associations of authenticity and identity through tradition and origin.[7]

Today, craft complements industrial practices as an independent and progressive economic activity. In the realm of timber construction, the carpentry trade has not perished; instead it has learned and benefited from industry by adopting modern business models and strategies that facilitate adjustment to changing market conditions. Mechanized and automated tools have reduced the amount of physical effort while increasing efficiency and precision. Medium-sized, regional carpentry operations employ serial production processes and computer-controlled machinery for the fabrication of large and complex building components, which are transported and assembled with the assistance of heavy equipment.[8] Emerging digital technologies and traditional craftsmanship do not contradict, but rather complement each other. This has allowed the introduction of new design and fabrication methods, which are closely guided by highly trained and experienced staff with intimate knowledge of the material's properties. Even though the work process has been fragmented into many individual steps due to its growing complexity, the carpenter has to maintain a holistic understanding of the entire process in order not to be relegated to the role of mere machine operator.[9] These new manufacturing technologies have not eroded craft, but rather require the training and integration of highly qualified personnel who are committed, can work autonomously, and take pride in their work. Skill and intellect, which had become separated in the process of industrialization, have been reunited, while craftsmanship will continue to assert its significance in shaping a new timber construction culture in the post-industrial era.

1 Pöschl, Wolfgang. "Handwerk – noch oder für immer?" *Zuschnitt: Zeitschrift über Holz als Werkstoff und Werke in Holz* 13.50 (2013). 22.   2 Hausenblas, Michael. "Die Sehnsucht nach dem Handwerk in Zeiten digitaler Omnipräsenz." *Zuschnitt: Zeitschrift über Holz als Werkstoff und Werke in Holz* 15.60 (2015). 27.   3 Sennett, Richard. *The Craftsman.* New Haven: Yale University Press, 2008. 20–21.   4 Aicher, Florian. "Proven by Time and Inspired – The New Craftsmanship." *Building with Timber: Paths into the Future.* Eds. Hermann Kaufmann and Winfried Nerdinger. Munich: Prestel, 2011. 202.   5 Sennett, Richard. 21.   6 Aicher, Florian. 202.   7 Hausenblas, Michael. 27.   8 Pöschl, Wolfgang. 22.   9 Kaiser, Gabriele. "Von der Hand in den Kopf und im Blick das Ganze: Die Handwerkskultur der Familie K." *Zuschnitt: Zeitschrift über Holz als Werkstoff und Werke in Holz* 7.26 (2007). 9.

1

2

3

4

1 Carpenters in the shop　2 Digital technologies and
traditional craftsmanship complement each other
3 Highly skilled carpenters translate drawings into
components for buildings　4 Modern carpentry
shop　5 Carpenter in the shop

5

Authenticity and Contradiction

For a large portion of the world's population, wood has always played an integral role in everyday life. It has served as a reliable energy source for heating and cooking, it has been used for construction, and its versatility has allowed it to be shaped into a variety of utensils and devices. Throughout history, wood's unique qualities have been fully recognized and accepted, and craftspeople and builders have learned to work with both its strengths and limitations. It has long been acknowledged that wood exposed to the elements will weather, while wooden surfaces subjected to common use will wear. This value system began to erode with increasing industrialization, when wood was gradually replaced in many applications by newly emergent mass-produced materials that appeared to be superior and more durable. The use of wood in building construction soon came to be considered rural and old-fashioned – it no longer fit into the worldview of a society striving for a modern, urban lifestyle. The exterior of log structures and timber frame houses was therefore often disguised beneath plaster to resemble middle-class stone and masonry buildings. Indoors, paint was frequently used to coat untreated wood-paneled walls and ceilings, both to conceal the signs of aging and to avoid associations with rural life.[1]

As soon as technological progress made it possible to readily control the properties of wood, mankind's relationship with wood was once again challenged, and as a result it has become ambiguous today.[2] While society has rediscovered wood's aesthetic qualities and appreciates them, it typically employs all means available to halt or slow wood's inherent, natural aging processes. The ephemeral character of wood is accepted, but everything possible is done to ensure its perpetuity. Even after it has been harvested and dried, wood continues to shrink and expand as it releases or absorbs moisture, exhibiting characteristics of a material that is alive – a fact that is not always met with great enthusiasm. The uniqueness and authenticity of wood is valued, yet imperfections including knotholes, cracks, and discolorations are considered undesirable by many, leading to the use of technology to ensure uniformity and homogeneity.

It is therefore no surprise that this ambivalence has led to wood being imitated more frequently than other materials. New synthetic plastic laminates developed in the 1950s provided the ability to preserve the appearance of natural wood grain while promoting durability, hygienic qualities, and ease of maintenance.[3] Wood was often subjected to skeuomorphism, a process in which a derivative object is made from an alternative material, but it retains ornamental design cues that were necessary features in the original. It was employed to evoke familiarity with the goal of making a new design more accessible and acceptable to users. With regard to wood, this resulted in the application of simulated wood grain to all kinds of modern consumer goods including furniture, appliances, and even cars.[4] Today, faux wood products in the form of beams, columns, paneling, and flooring are sometimes used for interior applications to satisfy people's desire for rusticality and *gemütlichkeit,* which can be described as "coziness." Even the use of real wood veneer for furniture and millwork can be considered imitation, since thin layers of highly valuable species are laminated onto inexpensive panels of lower-grade engineered wood to generate the appearance of solid wood. In this context, it is particularly ironic that present-day artificial wood laminates for various surface applications – and even products like ceramic tiles – attempt to emulate wood's natural characteristics, including knots and color variations, as convincingly as possible, while real wood veneers for high-end applications frequently strive for ultimate consistency without any noticeable flaws.[5] Going further, real wood is being manipulated to an equal extent in new ways, blurring its natural aesthetic qualities. Composite wood veneers are made from fast-growing trees from managed forests that have been sliced, dyed, and glued into artificial logs. These logs are processed through conventional means, resulting in an array of veneers, from those that look like standard wood veneers to others that are highly figured and colored with vaguely familiar yet new and unexpected visual traits.

In many cultures, the perception of the use of wood in construction continues to be shaped by vernacular architecture, traditional timber structures, and its stereotypical old-fashioned, rustic image. This notion has been especially disseminated by the Alpine kitsch architecture of the tourism industry, which although often fake, appeals to large numbers of visitors and satisfies expectations of a cozy and rustic experience. While wood has been widely accepted as a luxury finish for lining interiors such as executive offices and boardrooms, its use as a fully fledged modern building material is still challenged by the timeless appearance promised by glass, steel, and concrete. Today there is a breadth of timber products and construction techniques suited to a wide range of building applications. They are contextual, versatile, and progressive, enabling the return of a material that has been dismissed for a long time. They offer a contemporary aesthetic and honest use of materials that allow the expression of wood's unique qualities while addressing people's desire for tradition and authenticity in an increasingly technical and bewildering world. Going forward, the extent to which raw, natural, and ephemeral wood is accepted and appreciated needs to be continually negotiated within society, while keeping environmental, economic, and cultural concerns in mind.

1 Sagmeister, Rudolf, and Kathleen Sagmeister. *Holzbaukunst in Vorarlberg.* Bregenz: Eugen-Ruß-Verlag, 1988. 35. **2** Rinke, Mario. "Konstruktive Metamorphosen – Holz als immerwährendes Surrogat." *Holz: Stoff oder Form.* Eds. Mario Rinke and Joseph Schwartz. Sulgen: Niggli, 2014. 263–277. **3** Tschofen, Bernhard. "Über Totenbretter und andere Listen gegen die Vergänglichkeit." *Zuschnitt: Zeitschrift über Holz als Werkstoff und Werke in Holz* 1.4 (2001). 6–8. **4** Moravánskzy, Ákos. "Holzwege der Identität – Material und Stoffwechsel." *Holz: Stoff oder Form.* Eds. Mario Rinke and Joseph Schwartz. Sulgen: Niggli, 2014. 95–115. **5** Isopp, Anne. "Ein Plastikstuhl aus Holz." *Zuschnitt: Zeitschrift über Holz als Werkstoff und Werke in Holz* 8.32 (2008). 18.

1 Skeuomorphism: wood veneer applied to car
2 Faux wood beam made of polystyrene for decorative purposes   3 Composite wood veneers introduce new aesthetic qualities   4 Real wood veneers strive for ultimate consistency   5 Alpine kitsch architecture, Courchevel ski resort, France.   6 Contemporary solid wood interior: honest and authentic use of materials. Community Center St. Gerold, Austria. Architect: Cukrowicz Nachbaur Architekten.

5

6

Weathering and Preservation

As a natural material, wood continues to change even after it has been harvested, sawn, dried, converted into building products, and incorporated into structures. A building's occupants, the local climate, UV radiation, and pollutants gradually affect exposed wood, and the associated visible aging of surfaces can be a highly controversial topic. While the look of weathered and worn wood is readily accepted by some cultures, it is not necessarily embraced enthusiastically by all members of the general public. Its use as a building material is increasing, particularly in urban environments, and the exterior appearance of wood buildings in the long term will influence the popularity of timber construction in the future.

Attempts to protect and preserve wood are virtually as old as the use of wood itself, with early examples dating from Greek and Roman times. For centuries, preventative measures were the primary means employed to extend wood's serviceable life. This included the careful selection of durable species, determining the right time for harvest, thorough drying, correct processing, and appropriate architectural detailing. Trial and error methods were utilized by craftspeople over hundreds of years, their expertise accumulating as it was passed down from generation to generation – and it is this that continues to serve as the basis for the proper handling of wood in building applications today. Following these rules allowed the construction of timber structures that were able to stand the test of time, providing sufficient evidence that the notion of wood as a short-lived building material is misconceived. Well-preserved Austrian farmhouses from the 17th century still exist, the oldest remaining Norwegian stave churches were built in the 12th century, and some Japanese monuments date from as far back as 800 CE, making them some of the oldest surviving wooden buildings in the world.[1] Even though chemical coatings and wood preservatives were introduced during the Industrial Revolution in the 19th century, preventative measures continue to be the most effective way to protect wood.

Wood used on the exterior is subjected to a variety of environmental effects caused by sunshine, wind, rain, snow, hail, and other factors. The intensity of exposure is governed by a surface's orientation and inclination, as well as the regional climate, which is determined by geographical location and elevation.[2] Untreated wood that is exposed to the elements changes in texture and color over time. Photochemical, biological, and physical processes alter the chemical composition of wood surfaces and, in the worst cases, can lead to decay. Prolonged exposure to ultraviolet light degrades the lignin in wood, which is an organic polymer responsible for binding the cellulose fibers together. The discoloration that results can range from a reddish-yellow to a dark brown tone depending on the intensity and duration of the radiation. The decomposed lignin is soluble in water and may therefore be dissolved and washed out by driving rain, leaving behind the white cellulose fibers. Moisture from dew and precipitation encourages the growth of microorganisms such as stain and mold fungi, which leads to the familiar graying of wood. Depending on the environmental factors involved, however, this color change does not occur evenly and so it can initially cause a blotchy appearance, taking several years to produce a more attractive silvery-gray patina.[3] This is particularly the case if protruding building elements, such as roof overhangs, awnings, and windowsills, partially protect the wood surfaces below from direct exposure. If even weathering is desired, it is advisable to avoid projections and highly articulated facades, so as to achieve a relatively consistent transition from brown to light gray and then to dark gray tones.[4] As long as there is no decay present, these physical changes do not affect the strength of the wood, and all untreated wood surfaces, regardless of the species, undergo the same transformative process. This applies equally to low-grade softwoods from boreal and temperate forests and to high-quality tropical hardwoods.

A variety of surface treatments are used to prevent aging and these can also influence the exterior appearance of timber buildings. Stains, lacquers, and paints contain pigments to impart color. The UV protection offered by these pigments can effectively protect wood from the degradation caused by the short-wave solar radiation that initiates the aging process. Coatings also reduce the absorption of rainwater and moisture and thereby minimize the amount of surface cracking experienced by wood. They further provide physical protection from dirt, hail, and driving rain.[5] The level of pigmentation in a coating significantly affects its durability. Solid-color paints and lacquers are highly pigmented and produce very long-lasting finishes, but they usually form a continuous, opaque film that obscures the natural color and grain of wood. Semi-transparent stains allow the texture and grain of wood to remain visible, but only products that contain iron oxide pigments are able to block sufficient amounts of UV radiation.[6] While transparent coatings might act as a water repellent, they are not suitable for exterior applications in most cases, since their lack of pigment means that they do not offer any UV protection.[7] In order to circumvent a prolonged period of uneven coloring, exterior surfaces are sometimes pre-treated with a finish to simulate the appearance of weathered wood. As the applied coating degrades and wears off over time, the grayed wood below is revealed, resulting in a uniform and less noticeable transition to its ultimate aged look. Despite their ability to protect wood, coatings and finishes are subject to deterioration through weathering, so they require regular inspection, maintenance, and reapplication. It is important to note that surface treatments cannot compensate for the selection of incorrect materials and the failure to implement preventative measures during the design phase. Also, careful selection of the most suitable coating for a particular application is critical, since it determines aging and appearance over time, functionality and durability, and ultimately customer satisfaction.

The growth of decay-producing fungi only occurs if wood is continuously saturated with water in the presence of oxygen and its moisture content remains above 20 percent over prolonged periods of time. Appropriate architectural design can ensure that exposed surfaces only undergo superficial changes that affect their aesthetic appearance, but not their functionality. Construction details that either keep building components dry or promote their quick drying out will reduce the likelihood of infestation by wood-destroying fungi and insects. Best practices include raising wooden facades high enough above adjacent horizontal surfaces to prevent damage caused by splashing water, providing roof overhangs and protrusions that minimize the effects of direct weathering, and covering horizontal and minimally sloping wood surfaces with waterproof materials to avoid contact with standing water.[8] While the possibilities of taking these preventative measures should be exhausted first, the circumstances are sometimes such that the wood cannot be kept dry, so additional action needs to be taken. Since certain woods are more durable than others under exposure to moisture for extended periods, the selection of a naturally rot-resistant wood species can offer a viable solution. In particular, many tropical hardwoods are less prone to decay, but their use is considered controversial in the majority of cases, due to their limited availability and the questionable practices often employed in their sourcing. They are undoubtedly some of the most durable woods in the world and can at times be acquired from certified forests, but locally available species such as redwood, western red cedar, black locust, chestnut, and oak may possess very similar properties and can frequently be readily obtained from sustainably managed sources. A suitable alternative is thermal modification, which involves the heating of wood in the absence of oxygen to induce changes to its chemical structure. This process increases wood's dimensional stability by reducing its ability to absorb water, while enhancing its biological resistance to wood-destroying fungi and insects. The process leads to a darkening of the wood's surface, but it has the advantages that it can be employed for any species and does not require the use of chemicals. The main shortcoming of thermally modified wood is its decreased strength, which means that its application for load-bearing purposes is limited.

Rotting does not occur if wood is completely submerged under water, since decay-producing fungi need oxygen to flourish. Above ground, if saturation leads to a moisture content of more than 20 percent for prolonged periods of time, treatment with a chemical wood preservative is usually the only option to provide sufficient protection. The most common non-pressure treatment methods include brushing, spraying, dipping, and soaking. Pressure treatment processes such as vacuum pressure impregnation, however, tend to achieve higher absorption rates, leading to deeper and more uniform penetration. Oil-borne preservatives have mostly been replaced by waterborne products, which are odorless, easy to cover with paint, and less hazardous to the environment. Effective protection is provided by a combination of various chemical compounds including copper, chromium, arsenic, ammonium, and borate.[9] Recent years have seen the emergence of new treatment methods, which have been marketed as non-toxic alternatives to conventional approaches. Acetylation is a process that chemically modifies wood through the use of acetic acid, greatly increasing its dimensional stability, resistance to fungal and insect infestation, and paint retention. Acetylated wood retains excellent strength properties, which makes it highly suitable for structural applications. Another recent development is furfurylation, which involves the impregnation of wood with furfuryl alcohol (produced from a bio-based liquid), followed by a curing phase. After treatment, the wood exhibits improved resistance to microbial decay and insect attack as well as increased stability and hardness, without containing any toxins and chemicals.[10]

There is no doubt that surface coatings and chemical preservatives improve the life expectancy of wooden building components. They are often the only way to facilitate the utilization of many native species, which otherwise would have to be replaced with more carbon-intensive, less ecologically friendly building materials. The use of preservatives to protect wood does, however, raise environmental concerns and is often controversial. As a building material, wood is particularly valued for its recyclability and reusability, but these benefits are severely curtailed if coatings and impregnations are used. The durability of wood surfaces in exterior settings is not only influenced by environmental conditions and the species, but it is also highly dependent on proper design, detailing, execution, and maintenance. The possibilities of preventative measures should be sufficiently exhausted before resorting to chemical treatments, and even then, these should be used sparingly.

1 Peer, Johann. "Holzschutz an den Bauernhäusern des Bregenzerwaldes." *Zeitschrift über Holz als Werkstoff und Werke in Holz* 5.21 (2006). 4–6; "Urnes Stave Church." – *UNESCO World Heritage Centre.* United Nations Educational, Scientific, and Cultural Organization. Web. 09 Mar. 2016; "Buddhist Monuments in the Horyu-ji Area." – *UNESCO World Heritage Centre.* United Nations Educational, Scientific, and Cultural Organization. Web. 09 Mar. 2016.   2 Schober, Klaus Peter, and Gerhard Grüll. "Fassade und Zeit." *Fassaden aus Holz.* By Klaus Peter Schober et al. Vienna: proHolz Austria, 2010. 9.   3 Sell, Jürgen, Jürg Fischer, and Urs Wigger. "Forschungspanorama: Oberflächenschutz von Holzfassaden." *Zeitschrift über Holz als Werkstoff und Werke in Holz* 1.4 (2001). 22–27.   4 Kaufmann, Hermann. "Hineinverwittern in die Landschaft." *Zeitschrift über Holz als Werkstoff und Werke in Holz* 1.4 (2001). 18–19.   5 Schober, Klaus Peter, and Gerhard Grüll. 9.   6 Grüll, Gerhard. "Oberflächenbehandlung von Holz im Außenbereich: Gestaltungsmittel mit Schutzfunktionen." *Zeitschrift über Holz als Werkstoff und Werke in Holz* 5.21 (2006). 10–13.   7 Sell, Jürgen, Jürg Fischer, and Urs Wigger. 22–27.   8 Sell, Jürgen, Jürg Fischer, and Urs Wigger. 22–27.   9 Lebow, Stan T. "Wood Preservation." *Wood Handbook: Wood as an Engineering Material.* Madison, WI: United States Department of Agriculture, Forest Service, Forest Products Laboratory, 2010. 15.1–15.28.   10 Grüll, Gerhard. "Coatings for Wood in Exterior Use." *Detail: Review of Architecture and Construction Details* Feb. 2012. 172–177.

2

3

4

5

6

1 Heddal Stave Church, Norway, 13th century
2 Farm houses, Austria   3 Urnes Stave Church,
Norway, 12th century   4 Weathered shingled
facade   5 Unevenly weathered facade   6 Uneven
weathering due to windowsill   7 Unevenly
weathered wood facade   8 Uneven weathering
of old barn facade due to roof overhang

7

8

9

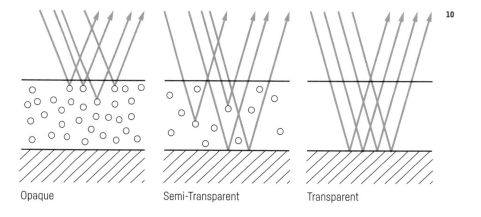

10

Opaque　　　　　Semi-Transparent　　　　　Transparent

11

12

13

9 Even silvery-gray patina on untreated shingled wood facade   **10** The level of pigmentation affects the ability of coatings to provide UV protection   **11** Coatings require regular visual inspection, maintenance, and reapplication   **12** Wood facade raised high enough above the ground to prevent damage by splashing water   **13** Protection of end grain   **14** Steel footing raises wood column high enough above the ground to prevent damage by splashing water   **15** Vacuum pressure impregnation of dimensional lumber

14

15

Health and Well-Being

The use of wood for construction offers numerous benefits that can positively affect the physical and mental wellness of a building's occupants. When structural timber components are exposed on the interior, or wood is applied to floor, wall, or ceiling surfaces, its distinctive properties can contribute to the creation of a healthy indoor climate, while its scent, warm appearance, and the natural feel of its surfaces can induce comfort and well-being. Such interiors benefit in equal measure from the aesthetic and physical qualities of wood, as a building material that is healthy, safe, and harmless when used properly and standard rules of practice are followed.

Wood can have a balancing effect on the moisture content of indoor environments. Its porosity allows the absorption of water vapor from the air, thus moderating any increase in relative humidity. Conversely, wood releases water vapor into the air when humidity levels get low. While this dynamic behavior can successfully regulate fluctuations of moisture content, it is only effective if the wooden surfaces remain untreated or if vapor-permeable coatings are used. Wood possesses lower thermal conductivity than other building materials, which means that it is perceived as warmer to the touch when compared with steel, concrete, stone, and masonry. Additionally, a space lined with wood provides largely homogeneous surface temperature levels, which contributes to the thermal comfort of its inhabitants.[1]

Concern for hygiene and cleanliness continues to limit the interior use of exposed and unfinished wood surfaces in favor of other finish materials. Recent studies have revealed, however, that wood possesses excellent antibacterial and antimicrobial characteristics, which are especially critical in healthcare environments or spaces that are used for food preparation. Due to wood's hygroscopic nature, its cells quickly absorb and bind liquids that would otherwise enable bacteria and microorganisms to survive and grow on its surface. In contrast, research has shown that a thin nutrient solution layer tends to linger on plastic, metal, and glass surfaces, serving as an ideal medium for germs.[2] In addition to the hygroscopic properties that are inherent to all woods, some species such as pine, oak, and larch contain high levels of extractives, which are substances that inherently prevent bacterial growth.[3] Wood therefore exhibits hygienic properties that are superior to those of many other building materials.

Highly insulated and airtight building envelopes have been developed in recent years to improve energy efficiency, often resulting in interior spaces with low air-exchange rates. This has led to increased concern about indoor air contamination with pollutants that are emitted by building materials, furniture, cleaning agents, and other sources. Largely responsible for these emissions are volatile organic compounds or vocs, which are a group of chemicals that includes terpenes, aldehydes, ketones, alkanes, carboxylic acids, and many others. The enormous quantity of VOCs in the indoor air, their variability, and their composition can make comprehensive toxicological assessments difficult. The effects on health can include eye, nose, and throat irritation, respiratory problems, nausea, fatigue, memory impairment, and loss of concentration. All these can be summarized under the term "sick building syndrome," a condition in which occupants exhibit acute health and comfort symptoms that are caused by time spent in buildings with poor indoor air quality.[4] This is aggravated by the fact that people in industrialized nations spend about 90 percent of their lives indoors.[5]

Natural wood also constitutes a source of VOCs. Softwoods such as spruce, pine, fir, and larch emit terpenes, which are responsible for their characteristic and mostly pleasantly perceived scents. Hardwoods, in general, contain considerably fewer VOCs than softwoods. While terpene content is insignificant in hardwoods, aldehydes and carboxylic acids dominate. Wood-based composite products exhibit emission profiles that are similar to those of solid wood, since dried and processed wood still contains volatile organic compounds. To date, research studies have not revealed any health risks associated with the VOCs specific to wood, but it is advisable to avoid particular wood species when employing certain types of construction systems.[6] When large areas of exposed wood are used – as is often the case in solid timber construction – building components should be free of the woods that, like pine, are highest in extractives, since these can emit correspondingly high quantities of terpenes and aldehydes, building up concentrations to levels that might exceed local standards of indoor air quality for extended periods of time.[7]

Additional emissions of VOCs can be caused by wood preservatives and coatings, as well as the glues used in wood-based composite products. The formaldehyde content of wood resins sparked a health and safety debate in the 1980s, but it is has become less controversial as manufacturers address these concerns. Urea-formaldehyde adhesives, which are commonly found in resins used for the production of particleboard and medium density fiberboard (MDF) for furniture, cabinetry, and architectural millwork, can release low concentrations of formaldehyde even when cured and should therefore be avoided. Structural wood products such as plywood, oriented strand board, and glued-laminated timber are sometimes manufactured with phenol-formaldehyde and melamine-formaldehyde adhesives. While formaldehyde is still present in these types of resin, they form highly stable bonds during pressing and do not off-gas after curing.[8] Some manufacturers offer products that are bonded using polyurethane (PUR), polymeric methylene diphenyl diisocyanate (PMDI), and polyvinyl acetate (PVA), which are formaldehyde-free resins.[9] Most adhesives used today for composite wood products have relatively low formaldehyde emission levels that either meet or are exempt from the world's leading formaldehyde emissions standards and regulations.[10] Even though the levels are now lower, appropriate air exchange rates are encouraged in order to avoid harmful concentrations of vocs in interior environments. Such accumulation is an increasing concern as energy conservation measures are resulting in buildings with more airtight envelopes.

Lastly, exposure to outdoor nature has been shown to have positive effects on human welfare, and its stress-reducing benefits have been scientifically well documented.[11] Levels of psychological well-being are measured in terms of objective parameters such as the vital signs and skin conductance levels, which change according to emotion and stress responses in the human body. Furthermore, recent pilot studies in North America, Europe, and Asia have established a link between the indoor use of wood and physical and mental health. These findings suggest that exposed wood surfaces can lower the reactivity of the sympathetic nervous system in the occupants of built environments. This is associated with reductions in parameters such as blood pressure, heart rate, psychological stress, and susceptibility to illness, together with improved ability to concentrate and perform creative tasks.[12] In longer-term studies, exposure to wood has been shown not only to prevent humans from becoming stressed, but also to lead to a decrease in stress levels and even to promote healing and recovery. These results reveal a clear relationship between the presence of wood and the physiological manifestations of reduced stress, and they offer opportunities to capitalize on the benefits that exposed wood may afford. While the use of wood in interiors can promote and enhance the physical and mental well-being of the occupants, the newness of the subject matter means that, as yet, not much psychophysiological research has been carried out into the effects of wood on health, so further and more extensive studies will be needed.[13]

1 Salthammer, Tunga, and Rainer Marutzky. *Bauen und Leben mit Holz*. Berlin: Informationsdienst Holz, 2013. 16–18.   **2** Krichmayr, Karin. "Hölzerne Lunge: von atemaktiv bis schmalbrüstig." *Zuschnitt: Zeitschrift über Holz als Werkstoff und Werke in Holz* 10.39 (2010). 18–19.   **3** Stingl, Robert, and Christian Hansmann. "Holz und Hygiene: Antibakterielle Eigenschaften von Materialien." *Zuschnitt: Zeitschrift über Holz als Werkstoff und Werke in Holz* 6.22 (2006). 12.   **4** Eichholzer, Astrid, Sabrina Niedermayer, and Gerald Aschacher. "VOC: Flüchtige organische Stoffe." *Zuschnitt: Zeitschrift über Holz als Werkstoff und Werke in Holz* 10.39 (2010). 23. **5** Klepeis, Neil E., William C. Nelson, Wayne R. Ott, John P. Robinson, Andy M. Tsang, Paul Switzer, Joseph V. Behar, Stephen C. Hern, and William H. Engelmann. "The National Human Activity Pattern Survey (NHAPS): A Resource for Assessing Exposure to Environmental Pollutants." *Journal of Exposure Analysis and Environmental Epidemiology* 11 (2001). 248.   **6** Salthammer, Tunga, and Rainer Marutzky. 22–25.   **7** Tappler, Peter. "Gesunde Raumluft im Büro." *Zuschnitt: Zeitschrift über Holz als Werkstoff und Werke in Holz* 16.61 (2016). 23.   **8** *Green Building Rating System Guides: Wood Specification: Indoor Air Quality*. ReThink Wood, 2014. **9** Fäh, Hanspeter, Bernhard Furrer, Beni Isenegger, Michael Pöll, and Roger Waeber. *Lignatec: Holzwerkstoffe in Innenräumen*. Zurich: Lignum, 2008.   **10** *Green Building Rating System Guides: Wood Specification: Indoor Air Quality*.   **11** *Wood and Human Health*. FPInnovations.   **12** Fell, David. "Healthy Building: The Case for Visual Wood." WoodWorks Online Webinar. July 2014.   **13** Augustin, Sally, and David Fell. *Wood as a Restorative Material in Healthcare Environments*. Pointe-Claire, QC: FPInnovations, 2015.

1

2

3

Exposed wood structure and surfaces: **1** Wood Innovation and Design Centre, Prince George, BC. Architect: Michael Green Architecture. **2** Forest Sciences Centre, University of British Columbia, Vancouver, BC. Architect: Dall-Lana Griffin Dowling Knapp Architects. **3 + 4** Université du Québec en Abitibi-Témiscamingue Science Pavilion, Rouyn-Noranda, Québec. Architect: BGLA, CCM2 Architects, TRAME Consortium. **5** Gymnasium, Seeheim, Germany. Architect: Loewer + Partner Architekten.

4

5

Wood in the City

Cities occupy only about 3 percent of the Earth's land surface.[1] For the first time in history, however, over half of the world's population lives in urban areas and this number is projected to rise to about 70 percent by 2050. The most urbanized regions today are North America, Latin America, and Europe. Africa and Asia, in contrast, have remained mostly rural, but they are expected to have the fastest population growth and pace of urbanization over the next decades.[2] In the second half of the 20th century, numerous cities in the industrialized countries went into decline as a significant percentage of the urban population moved out to the suburbs in search of a more affordable and convenient lifestyle. Recently however, the desire of younger generations to lead healthy and sustainable lives within vital and dense urban environments has increased, causing a reversal of this trend and the re-urbanization of inner cities. Additionally, high birth rates and lack of employment have forced many people in the rural areas of emerging countries to move to cities in the hope of better economic opportunities. Whatever the reason, most industrialized and developing nations will likely see a substantial increase in their urban populations, hand in hand with a greater need for sustainable and affordable housing. In many cities, the housing shortage has turned into a political issue, creating enormous pressure on municipalities to provide living space that simultaneously satisfies economic, ecological, and social concerns.[3]

Cities are undoubtedly responsible for contributing to anthropogenic climate change, since CO_2 emissions in urban regions are generally higher than in rural areas. However, carbon dioxide emissions are heavily based on settlement patterns, which means that compact and dense cities exhibit lower per-capita emission levels than sprawled and dispersed agglomerations. Dense cities largely owe their relatively low emissions and their energy efficiency to short travel distances, public transportation networks, and compact buildings with optimized surface-area-to-volume ratios that result in lower heating and cooling needs.[4] Given that the operational energy requirements of buildings have decreased over time, the next step in reducing greenhouse gas emissions is to lower their embodied energy content – the energy consumed in producing the materials for their construction. The utilization of wood for the primary structural system of buildings can play a critical role toward achieving this goal.

While wood was the most prevalent building material up to the 19th century, industrialization introduced new infrastructure, services, and building types that required the development of alternative construction concepts. Wood, with its seemingly unpredictable chemical and physical properties, was deemed unsuitable for these applications at the time, leading to the dominance of iron, steel, and reinforced concrete, which had been perfected through focused scientific research.[5] Today, the recent development of new composite wood products and timber construction technologies, along with amendments to building codes, has allowed wood to return to the city. While the number of urban timber buildings is currently limited to several pilot projects, new strategies for structural design, fire protection, and soundproofing have enabled the widespread construction of multi-story wood buildings that satisfy the most exacting building standards. Wood, a renewable resource, can be substituted for non-renewable building materials such as steel and concrete, decreasing reliance on fossil fuel-derived energy. This substitution can turn buildings into carbon sinks rather than sources of CO_2 emissions, effectively reducing their contribution to global warming. Additionally, the high degree of prefabrication in timber construction minimizes noise pollution and disruption at the jobsite, which is especially beneficial in densely populated urban settings. Off-site fabrication also leads to a reduction of particulate matter emissions, which has become an issue of increasing concern in inner-city environments. Furthermore, the natural qualities of wood can contribute to the comfort and well-being of urban dwellers, thus satisfying their desire for healthy and sustainable living.

The use of wood as a construction material in the city can be highly controversial, in particular with regard to its aesthetic integration into the cityscape. A timber structure, however, does not necessarily have to be recognizable as such on the exterior, and it can be clad in finishes that are better suited for its particular setting. The many historic urban timber buildings with masonry or stone-clad facades offer ample proof of this. In any case, "pure" timber structures with exposed surfaces are often not feasible due to the requirements imposed by local fire codes, and many applications will require hybrid structural systems in which wood is combined with concrete, steel, or other materials. Such innovations in timber construction offer fresh opportunities to create architecturally successful solutions that fit into the urban fabric.[6]

Since most of the world's population growth will be concentrated in cities, sustainable urban development will need to focus on the use of renewable energy and resources, the reduction of emissions, and the creation of healthy environments for living and working. Many cities around the world, among them Vienna, Munich, Zurich, London, and Vancouver, have therefore developed strategies and regulations to promote the use of wood in construction. This not only applies to residential buildings, but also to mixed-use developments and public buildings, including city halls, schools, and daycare centers. Although the use of wood in urban settings is still in its infancy, the continued development of timber construction technologies, accompanied by changes in building legislation, will further facilitate the return of wood to the city as a truly renewable and CO_2-neutral building material.

1 "The Growing Urbanization of the World." News Archive. The Earth Institute at Columbia University. Web. 03 Apr. 2016.　**2** *World Urbanization Prospects: The 2014 Revision, Highlights (ST/ESA/SER.A/352)*. New York: United Nations, Department of Economic and Social Affairs, Population Division, 2014. 1.　**3** *Mehrgeschossiges Bauen und Nachverdichtung in der Stadt: Fachtagung Holzbau in Hannover*. Berlin: Informationsdienst Holz, 2014. 7.　**4** Rode, Philipp, and Dimitri Zenghelis. "Die Zukunft ist grün." *Zuschnitt: Zeitschrift über Holz als Werkstoff und Werke in Holz* 15.59 (2015). 22.　**5** Cheret, Peter, and Arnim Seidel. "Der neue Holzbau." *Handbuch und Planungshilfe Urbaner Holzbau*. Eds. Peter Cheret, Kurt Schwaner, and Arnim Seidel. Berlin: DOM, 2013. 8–15.　**6** Kaufmann, Hermann. "Das Holz muss in die Stadt." *Zuschnitt: Zeitschrift über Holz als Werkstoff und Werke in Holz* 15.59 (2015). 4–5.

1-3 Increasing urbanization: London, Hong Kong, and Rio de Janeiro

4

5

6

7

8

9

4–6 9-story mass timber building. Murray Grove, London, 2009. Architect: Waugh Thistleton Architects. Engineer: Techniker.   **7 + 8** Multi-family mass timber development. Dalston Lane, London. Architect: Waugh Thistleton Architects. Engineer: Ramboll.   **9** Mass timber construction. Tamedia Headquarters, Zurich. Architect: Shigeru Ban Architects. Engineer: Creation Holz GmbH.   **10** University of East Anglia Blackdale Student Residence, Norwich. Architect: LSI Architects. Engineer: Ramboll.   **11** Wagramer Strasse Housing, Vienna. Architect: Schluder Architektur, Hagmüller Architekten. Engineer: RWT Plus ZT GmbH.

10   **11**

Building in Existing Fabric

Since most cities around the world are expected to experience considerable growth, creative solutions will be needed to accommodate the increasing population. Densely populated urban areas do not often possess sizable tracts of land that would allow the creation of entirely new neighborhoods. In contrast to green-field land on the outskirts, whose development ultimately contributes to urban sprawl, existing inner-city districts and buildings have great potential for modernization and redensification. Many outdated and convoluted apartment units no longer satisfy the needs of their tenants, and many buildings constructed in the second half of the 20th century do not meet current energy standards and are correspondingly expensive to operate. Today's timber construction systems can easily be tailored to furnish comprehensive solutions for the refurbishment of buildings, resulting in high-quality living spaces and substantial energy savings. Renovation projects not only capitalize on the readily available urban infrastructure, but they also take advantage of the embodied energy that is contained in the existing building stock. Tapping into the reserves that exist rather than adding new structures can make more efficient use of the resources a city has to offer.[1]

Within the dense urban fabric, construction with prefabricated timber elements offers a number of advantages that make them suitable for a wide range of applications. Extensions and infill developments are facilitated by the rapid erection and assembly of components, while minimizing noise pollution and disruption to neighbors. A high degree of prefabrication can optimize the workflow and mitigate space constraints on site. Rooftop additions consisting of one or more stories are often possible on top of historic buildings since these frequently possess considerable structural reserves. Wood also has a better strength-to-weight ratio than other materials, which results in comparatively lower dead loads acting on the structure below. The interior of an existing structure can be efficiently converted through the insertion of prefabricated, lightweight, and easily transportable timber elements. In such cases, wood's ease of workability with simple tools allows the straightforward adjustment on site of new components to the existing situation.

Since buildings completed between the 1950s and the 1980s consume high amounts of energy and make up a large portion of today's building stock, one of the greatest tasks going forward will be to increase their energy efficiency.[2] Improving the thermal performance of their envelopes can lower heating and cooling needs while making a significant contribution to the reduction of CO_2 emissions into the atmosphere. Current methods for envelope refurbishment often involve the use of exterior insulation and finish systems (EIFS), which predominantly utilize insulation materials made from mineral fiber or synthetic foam. These need large quantities of energy to produce, can be harmful to human health during installation, and are potentially hazardous to the environment, making them difficult to dispose of at the end of their service life. Conventional refurbishment practices also entail the inefficient cutting and processing of small-format insulation panels on site, which causes high levels of dust and noise emissions while generating large amounts of waste.[3] This can be very economical, due to low material costs, but the ecological effects are often neglected. When the various options are subjected to a comprehensive life-cycle analysis, viable alternatives using timber construction systems emerge as potentially more environmentally friendly.

Highly insulated timber panels can be prefabricated in the shop as single elements of story height or even full building height. They usually include insulation, air barriers and vapor retarders, doors, windows, interior finishes, and sometimes even exterior cladding. Additionally, heating, ventilation, and air conditioning systems, as well as photovoltaic panels, and solar thermal collectors, can easily be integrated. Such panels can either be placed in front of the existing facade, or they can replace the old building envelope after it has been removed. The loads from these timber panels are commonly transferred to the primary structure, while any remaining cavities are filled with insulating material. Modern measurement technologies, including tacheometry, photogrammetry, and 3D laser scanning, are employed to capture the existing building's geometry. This collected data serves as a basis for a three-dimensional model that is used throughout for design, fabrication, and assembly, thus ensuring that the custom-made timber panels fit precisely. While the initial effort tends to be greater than with conventional refurbishment methods, a thorough planning process accounts for all phases of the project, including transportation and installation. The use of large-format elements reduces on-site construction time, which minimizes the disruption of day-to-day use for occupants. This is particularly critical in the case of multi-family residences and public buildings, including schools, daycare centers, and administrative facilities, which often have to be refurbished while fully occupied.[4]

Their capacity for standardization, precision, and quality makes timber construction systems well suited for both the refurbishment of existing structures and the redensification of cities. Among their numerous advantages are adaptability, a high degree of prefabrication, shortened construction time, and lower weight and environmental impact than other building materials. In the light of climate change, efforts to further reduce CO_2 emissions caused by the existing building stock will continue to play a vital role, leading to a greater range of opportunities for the use of wood in densely populated urban areas.

1 Lattke, Frank. "Timber Building amidst Existing Structures." *Building with Timber: Paths into the Future.* Eds. Hermann Kaufmann and Winfried Nerdinger. Munich: Prestel, 2011. 78–81.　**2** Lattke, Frank. 78–81.　**3** Lattke, Frank. "Zukunftsfähig: Holz und Holzwerkstoffe in der energetischen Gebäudemodernisierung." *Zuschnitt: Zeitschrift über Holz als Werkstoff und Werke in Holz* 9.34 (2009). 9–11.　**4** Siegele, Klaus. "TES EnergyFacade: Sanieren mit vorgefertigten Holzrahmenelementen." *Zuschnitt: Zeitschrift über Holz als Werkstoff und Werke in Holz* 11.43 (2011). 22–23.

Extension

Infill

Rooftop Addition

Insertion

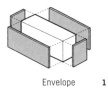
Envelope

1

2

3

4

5

1 Interventions in existing fabric   **2** Urban infill project.
C13, Berlin. Architect: Kaden Klingbeil Architekten.
Engineer: Pirmin Jung.   **3 + 4** Rooftop addition under
protective tent cover during construction. Treehouses
Bebelallee, Hamburg. Architect: blauraum Architekten
GmbH.   **5 + 6** Installation of prefabricated elements
to improve thermal performance. Grüntenstrasse,
Augsburg. Architect: lattkearchitekten. Engineer: bauart
Konstruktions GmbH & Co KG.

6

7

7–9 Existing building dating from 1958 in original condition, and after facade refurbishment. Infrared ther-
mography reveals the improvement of facade insulation
for the refurbished building compared with another
existing building in the background. GWG Fernpass-
strasse, Munich. Architect: Kaufmann. Lichtblau.
Architekten BDA. Engineer: merz kley partner ZT GmbH.

8

9

Multi-Story Timber Construction

Parts of Europe and Asia have long-standing traditions of erecting multi-story timber buildings, many of which have endured for centuries. Often using log or
timber frame construction techniques, some of them reach heights of four or
five stories, or even more. As a construction material, wood was largely displaced during the 19th century by steel, which was superseded in its turn by
concrete at the beginning of the 20th century. While multi-story timber construction disappeared altogether in most parts of the world during that time,
platform framing remained popular in North America and Northern Europe.[1]
The oil and energy crises in the 1970s led to the realization that previous technical advancements in the construction industry had come at the expense of
the environment, and the need became apparent for the development of more
sustainable strategies. This raised interest in the use of renewable energy and
materials, allowing wood construction to re-emerge as a possible solution. In
keeping with historic heavy timber construction precedents, frame systems
were initially employed, but panel systems based on the prevalent platform
framing technique soon followed. Over the last thirty years, machine stress rating has significantly improved the quality of dimensional lumber, while new
high-performance engineered wood products and fasteners have emerged.[2]
These technological innovations have led architects, engineers, and clients to
accept timber buildings increasingly as a viable solution.

Until recently, there was no demand for new structural solutions for mid-rise and
high-rise buildings. Throughout the modernist period, cities around the world
were dominated by steel and concrete. Considerable knowledge of these materials' structural performance, including their exposure to high seismic and
wind loads, has been acquired over time, along with an understanding of how
to protect them in the event of fire. This has made steel and concrete the construction materials of choice, allowing buildings to reach new heights that were
inconceivable just a few decades ago.[3] Tall buildings in particular pose a unique
dilemma, since they have both positive and negative environmental effects. On
the one hand, they increase density in inner-city environments, which makes
effective use of limited space. In moderate numbers, they promote mass public transport, thus reducing transport-related carbon dioxide emissions. Their
lower surface-area-to-volume ratios compared with single-family residences
allow them to be more energy-efficient, and they can be connected to district
heating and cooling systems that provide energy more effectively to a large
number of buildings in urban cores. On the other hand, these advantages have
to be set against the higher carbon dioxide emissions caused by the production
of the materials used to construct tall buildings. In general, the load-bearing
structure is responsible for the largest portion of a building's embodied energy,
and since high-rise buildings require proportionately more structural material, their carbon footprints also tend to be substantially higher (per square foot

or per square meter) than low-rise buildings.[4] Increasing the density of cities has become an important tool for combating climate change, however, and this inevitably means increasing building heights. Against this background, wood, with its ability to sequester large amounts of carbon, represents a solution for building tall structures that can turn cities bit by bit into carbon sinks.

Since fire safety is usually the biggest concern when building with timber, it is important to note the differences in fire performance between conventional light frame construction techniques and the new solid timber construction systems available today. The structural members in light frame construction are relatively small in size, making them more likely to ignite and collapse early in a fire. They are therefore protected with a fire-resistant barrier such as gypsum board, which creates, in effect, an arrangement of compartments containing concealed combustible material. In contrast, construction with mass timber beams, columns, and panels typically does not yield such configurations, which greatly reduces the risk of a concealed fire. These members also perform extremely well due to their solid nature, which makes them inherently able to resist fire without any additional protection. Their substantial mass allows a char layer to form on the surface, insulating the remaining wood from heat penetration and ignition. Although the charred portion no longer has any structural strength, the non-charred section retains its structural capacity over an extended period of fire exposure. As a result, the fire-resistance rating and thus the required dimensions of large timber members can easily be determined, since the thickness of the protective sacrificial layer can be calculated using charring rates that have been established through fire tests. This unique characteristic also makes solid timber more predictable in a fire than steel, which will deform and collapse quickly above particular temperature thresholds. Even though it is considered to be a non-combustible material, steel must be protected through additional fireproofing. As an alternative to reliance on the charring behavior described above, mass timber members can be protected through encapsulation with fire-rated gypsum board or other non-combustible materials in order to satisfy building code regulations. The addition of automatic fire-suppression systems such as sprinklers, fire alarms, and detectors can often satisfy fire-resistance requirements without the need for encapsulation, thus allowing exposed surfaces that showcase wood's natural qualities.

The permissible maximum heights for combustible buildings vary widely from country to country. Light wood frame construction projects in North America, for example, may reach five to six stories. The market for solid timber construction has developed more rapidly in Europe than in other parts of the world, since strong regulatory policies support the use of renewable resources, low carbon-content building materials, and energy-efficient construction.[5] While the height is still restricted by the building code in many countries, some nations, including the United Kingdom, Italy, Finland, Sweden, and Norway, impose no specific height limits as long as certain standards of safety can be demonstrated.[6] Instead of enforcing traditional prescriptive building codes that are based on recognized standards of good practice, the respective jurisdictions specify performance requirements without prescribing specific measures to fulfill them. These performance-based building codes allow architects and engineers to develop customized fire-protection strategies in order to satisfy the specified criteria, which frequently necessitates the fire testing of individual building assemblies. Many countries have adapted their fire regulations over time as the understanding of mass timber buildings and their behavior in the event of fire has increased.[7]

Tall buildings often contain residential units, so building components such as floors and walls have to provide sufficient sound insulation from both outside and inside noise sources. Due to its greater mass, solid timber construction generally offers better acoustic control of both airborne and impact sound transmission than light frame construction does. Since mass timber elements by themselves do not often meet the necessary acoustic requirements, sound-absorbing insulation and cavities are typically added. Careful attention to detailing is essential in order to achieve satisfactory acoustic performance. This includes sealing gaps to avoid sound leaks, utilizing materials with absorptive properties and sufficient mass, installing resilient connectors between individual layers within assemblies, and ensuring the discontinuity of structural components to minimize flanking sound transmission.

Wood can serve as a competitive alternative to steel and concrete for the design of tall buildings due to its excellent strength-to-weight ratio. This also means that it places less of a dead load on the structure and foundations, making it particularly suitable for soils with low bearing capacity. The higher a building is, the greater the lateral loads caused by wind become. In tall structures, it is therefore crucial to create an effective lateral load-resisting system, for which the rigidity and dimensional stability of solid timber panels can offer an appropriate solution. Extensive testing has established that they also perform well in earthquakes and are well suited for seismically sensitive areas. While solid wood components tend to exhibit rigid and brittle characteristics, combining them with metal connectors allows them to achieve the ductile behavior and energy dissipation necessary for safe performance during seismic events. The minimal extent of any deformation and structural damage means that repairs can be made quickly, allowing the building to return to normal operation soon afterwards.[8]

Over the last decade, a number of pioneering architects, engineers, and clients have initiated a new building culture for multi-story timber construction around the world. This has been accompanied by comprehensive structural research, improvements in soundproofing, amendments to building codes, and the development of new building systems and wood products, in particular cross-laminated timber. Current design approaches include the use of frame construction, panel construction, and solid timber construction systems. Hybrid systems using timber in combination with steel and concrete are particularly popular, since they facilitate not only increased heights but also longer spans, thus enabling a variety of uses, including office and residential use. Since they are often free from any load-bearing interior walls, their layouts provide developers with a great deal of flexibility, which allows them to respond to changing market demand.[9] A number of mid-rise buildings have already been constructed in urban areas and projects up to twenty-four stories tall are on the drawing board. Several design teams have presented proposals for high-rise buildings with thirty or more stories, but these are still in the conceptual stages. Further design and engineering research is necessary before these heights can be achieved and building codes amended to allow the construction of such structures. As countries increasingly employ carbon pricing to manage global warming emissions, solid timber construction will most likely experience an upswing, since wood is less susceptible to energy price fluctuations and carbon emission penalties than other building materials are.[10] Within the construction industry, growing awareness of its contribution to climate change will continue to push the boundaries of building with timber in order to conserve energy, reduce carbon dioxide emissions, and create healthy indoor environments. Progressing urbanization will require tall buildings, and wood is expected to revolutionize mid-rise and high-rise construction in the future.

1 Kolb, Josef. *Systems in Timber Engineering.* Basel: Birkhäuser Verlag, 2008. 182. 2 Dederich, Ludger. "Mehrgeschossiger Holzbau – gestern und heute." *Handbuch und Planungshilfe Urbaner Holzbau.* Eds. Peter Cheret, Kurt Schwaner, and Arnim Seidel. Berlin: DOM, 2013. 38–45. 3 mgb ARCHITECTURE + DESIGN, Equilibrium Consulting, LMDG Ltd, and BTY Group. *The Case for Tall Wood Buildings.* Vancouver: 2012. 26–27. 4 Skidmore, Owings & Merrill, LLP. *Timber Tower Research Project.* Chicago: 2013. 2. 5 *Tall Wood Takes a Stand: Examining North America's evolution toward taller wood buildings.* ReThink Wood, 2014. 3–4. 6 Isopp, Anne. "So hoch darf man mit Holz bauen: Ein Ländervergleich." *Zuschnitt: Zeitschrift über Holz als Werkstoff und Werke in Holz* 15.59 (2015). 16–17. 7 Mayo, Joseph. *Solid Wood.* New York: Routledge, 2015. 38. 8 *Tall Wood Takes a Stand.* 4–5. 9 Kolb, Josef. 182–183. 10 mgb ARCHITECTURE + DESIGN, Equilibrium Consulting, LMDG Ltd, and BTY Group. II.

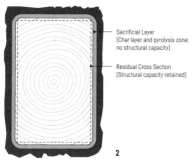

Sacrificial Layer
(Char layer and pyrolysis zone;
no structural capacity)

Residual Cross Section
(Structural capacity retained)

1 5-story log structure in Evolène, Switzerland
2 Charring of structural mass timber elements
3 + 4 Fire testing of CLT floor panel   **5** CLT panel after
fire testing. Char layer and pyrolysis zone are clearly
visible.   **6** 4-story timber building: H4, Bad Aibling,
Germany, 2010. Architect: Schankula Architekten. Engineer: bauart Konstruktions GmbH & Co KG.   **7** 8-story
mass timber building: Kampa K8, Aalen, Germany, 2014.
Architect: Florian Nagler Architekten GmbH. Engineer:
bauart Konstruktions GmbH & Co KG.   **8 + 9** 8-story
mass timber building: H8, Bad Aibling, Germany, 2011.
Architect: Schankula Architekten. Engineer: bauart
Konstruktions GmbH & Co KG.   **10** 7-story mass timber
structure: Wood Innovation and Design Centre, Prince
George, BC, 2014. Architect: Michael Green Architecture. Engineer: Equilibrium Consulting.

6

7

9

8

10

11

11 Concept for high-rise timber buildings in New York City by Michael Green Architecture   **12** 24-story timber tower in Vienna, scheduled for completion in 2017.   **13 + 14** Structural concept for a 30-story timber tower by Skidmore, Owings & Merrill

12

13

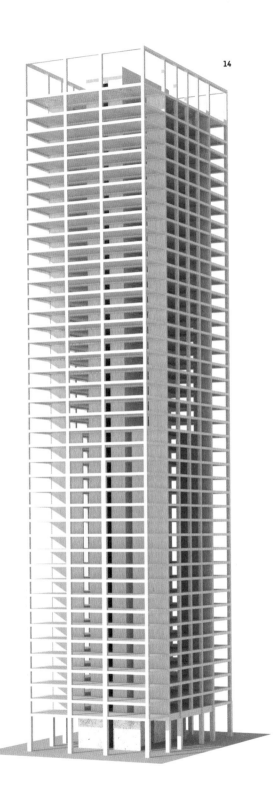

14

Rapid Housing

Severe natural catastrophes such as earthquakes, tsunamis, storms, and flooding test the limits of society and its built infrastructure. Simultaneously, man-made disasters are becoming a more common occurrence, with detrimental consequences. Not only do these events have the potential to cause extensive loss of human life, they can also result in large numbers of displaced and homeless people, who have to be accommodated. Tents are frequently used as a first response to provide shelter, due to the fact that they are inexpensive, lightweight, easy to assemble, and usually available worldwide. Their disadvantages become readily apparent when they have to be deployed for a prolonged duration, since they do not offer adequate protection from the elements, often leading conditions on the ground to worsen.[1] Having been faced with adversity, disaster victims should not be expected to live in makeshift shelters for extended periods of time. If all this is to be avoided, relief organizations and governmental agencies not only need to deliver immediate emergency assistance, but also need to offer long-term solutions that will allow the affected populations to resume their lives in a sustainable and dignified manner.

Timber construction has a history of providing accommodation quickly in a variety of situations. Prefabricated, transportable units made of wood were originally developed to house military personnel and field hospitals in 19th century Europe. However, they were soon adapted for civil purposes to help relieve the effects of war, epidemics, natural disasters, and economic crises. As many metropolitan areas struggled with the growth of their populations and sought to remedy housing shortages, mass-produced portable shelters became an effective means of coping with rapidly changing social circumstances.[2] Following the hardship experienced in the first half of the 20th century, mobile wood-framed housing units continued to be perceived as merely ephemeral buildings, and they failed to receive any further attention from a post-war society striving for prosperity. In light of the apparently growing frequency of natural and man-made disasters, the use of timber construction in relief efforts has experienced a resurgence in recent years. This can be attributed to its numerous benefits, including low carbon emissions, energy efficiency, availability, and durability, along with the ability to provide flexible floor plans and healthy indoor climates. High levels of prefabrication enable fast erection while facilitating construction year-round, independently of seasonal variation in the weather.[3] Integrated solutions include the provision of temporary shelters for refugees, the conversion of existing buildings into living spaces so as to address inner-city housing shortages, and the creation of large, multi-story, affordable housing developments for the permanent rehousing of displaced populations.[4]

Intensified by armed conflicts in Asia and Africa, the recent refugee crisis in Europe has highlighted the demand for adequate temporary quarters. This has aggravated an existing housing shortfall due to a lack of construction activity in years past. Many refugees have been obliged to stay in overcrowded accommodation on the edges of towns, often without any opportunity for interaction with the local community. Vacant schools, gymnasiums, and hotels have had to be repurposed as emergency shelters, while tent and container camps have been set up to satisfy the most basic needs. Container-based approaches are particularly prevalent, but their spatial and aesthetic characteristics tend to ignore cultural, social, and religious matters, making them more suitable as an interim solution.[5] In contrast, customized prefabricated timber construction systems allow the implementation of high-quality, durable, and sustainable accommodation that not only satisfies humanitarian and social concerns, but is constructed according to the latest environmental and energy efficiency standards. This facilitates their conversion into permanent housing at a later point in time, as well as allowing them to be relocated and reused for other purposes such as retirement homes, student dormitories, or daycare centers.[6] Successful concepts do not only provide initial shelter, they are also capable of fostering the long-term integration of refugees into the local community and job market.

1 *Spezial: Holzbau nach Katastrophenfällen.* Berlin: Informationsdienst Holz, 2006. 20.   2 Doßmann, Axel, Jan Wenzel, and Kai Wenzel. "Operative Architektur: Zur Geschichte transportabler Holzbaracken." *Zuschnitt: Zeitschrift über Holz als Werkstoff und Werke in Holz* 9.36 (2009). 18–19.   3 "Warum Holz? Vorteile der Holzbauweise." *Wohnraum für Flüchtlinge in Holzbauweise.* Deutscher Holzwirtschaftsrat e.V. (DHWR), Web. 14 Apr. 2016.   4 "Holzbaulösungen." *Holzbauten für Flüchtlinge.* Landesbetrieb Wald und Holz Nordrhein-Westfalen, Web. 14 Apr. 2016.   5 *Flüchtlinge brauchen Wohnungen, keine Behälter! Positionspapier zum Bau von Flüchtlingsunterkünften.* Wiesbaden: Architekten- und Stadtplanerkammer Hessen, 2015.   6 "Warum Holz? Vorteile der Holzbauweise."

1

2

3

4

5

1 Prefabrication of modules in the shop   **2** Assembly of modules on site   **3** Refugee housing, Steigertahlstrasse, Hanover. Architect: MOSAIK Architekten BDA.   **4 + 5** Prefabricated modular housing. Concept: Bauer Holzbausysteme.   **6 + 7** Prefabricated panel construction system provides housing for refugees. Concept: Wunderle + Partner Architekten mbB, Gumpp & Maier GmbH.

6

7

Regional Value Added

Over the last several decades, the industrialized nations have provided progressive
leadership in the development of innovative wood products and construction
systems. At the same time, globalization and technological advancements have
had a profound effect on their forestry and timber sectors. While strong global
competition has led to a growth of processing capacity, it has tended to favor
the formation of large, consolidated, and highly automated manufacturing operations, making it more difficult for smaller businesses to survive.[1] In general,
raw materials are increasingly sold on international markets rather than trad-
ed at local or regional levels. Entire logs are exported from the industrialized
nations to emerging economies for further processing, resulting in the simul-
taneous export of any added value that would otherwise have been retained
through the local production of goods. Rural, timber-dependent communities
have been particularly affected by the disruption of traditional process chains
and the disappearance of secondary manufacturing facilities. The associated
loss of employment opportunities has been accompanied by the forfeiture of
critical knowledge and expertise, which is then no longer available for innovation and new product development. This has weakened economically under-
developed areas even further, increasing their dependence on global markets.[2]

The advent of mass timber products such as cross-laminated timber for the construction of tall buildings has opened up new prospects for manufacturing
and for potential added value in rural regions with abundant timber resources,
additionally creating opportunities to connect them with urban communities.
While a number of regional initiatives have been encouraging timber construction to mitigate climate change for some time, many local and national governments are now also endorsing strategies to increase the use of wood, in order to
strengthen these rural economies. Their main objectives include the generation
of specialist expertise, the establishment of local manufacturing capabilities
and supply chains, the creation of new jobs, and the development of products
primarily for regional consumption, thus fostering the expansion of strong domestic markets. A region's forest and timber industry can be most effectively
promoted by utilizing the infrastructure of a "wood cluster," which is a network
of independent businesses, professional organizations, and educational institutions in the same or related fields. A fully developed cluster comprises all aspects
of the value chain, ranging from the extraction of resources to the marketing of
products and services, and its members cooperate with each other to generate
economic growth that is usually above the industry average. Internally, these
networks facilitate the exchange of knowledge and research, share job-train-
ing resources, ensure the availability of natural resources, and foster innovative
product development. Externally, they maintain public outreach programs with
the goal of expanding their customer base, explore domestic and international
market opportunities, and increase the productivity and competitive ability of

the participating businesses. A cluster usually operates within a clearly defined region, so it can take advantage of economies of scale, short transportation distances, and the concentration of expertise while enjoying the support of the local government, authorities, and public institutions.[3] Wood clusters already exist in several countries. Finland and Austria, for example, have well-established networks that can serve as models for other markets, even though they differ considerably in their focus. The forest cluster in Finland operates at a national scale with very specific economic targets, and it is closely tailored to large-scale industrial enterprises in the forest and timber industry, leaving little room for small and mid-sized business ventures.[4] It is comprised of machine and equipment manufacturers, logistics companies, energy producers, chemical manufacturers, the packaging industry, and research and higher education institutions.[5] Austria, on the other hand, possesses a number of regional clusters that concentrate on linking small and medium-sized wood-processing and manufacturing businesses with the goal of fostering collaboration, knowledge exchange, and product development as a means of ensuring that its members can remain highly productive and competitive in an increasingly global market.

Studies have shown that such dedicated networks can act as catalysts of regional value added, but trust and willingness to cooperate are required by all participants in order to capitalize on their full potential. Comprehensive strategies that promote local traditions and culture, provide employment and benefits, reduce the long-distance transportation of goods, and strengthen local economies can make an important contribution to sustainable development since they address social, ecological, and economic concerns.[6]

1 Gothe, Dorle, and Ulf Hahne. *Wald-Arbeitspapier Nr. 14: Regionale Wertschöpfung durch Holz-Cluster.* Eds. Siegfried Lewark and Edgar Kastenholz. Freiburg: Institut für Forstbenutzung und forstliche Arbeitswissenschaft, Universität Freiburg, 2005. 3. 2 Gothe, Dorle. *Regionale Wertschöpfung durch vermehrten Holzbau: Handlungsansätze für Kommunen & Akteure im Holzcluster.* Nettersheim: Wald und Holz Eifel e. V., 2015. 3–4. 3 Pöyry Forest Industry Consulting GmbH, Bayerische Landesanstalt für Wald und Forstwirtschaft, Deutsche Gesellschaft für Holzforschung, and Technische Universität München. *Cluster Forst und Holz in Bayern. Abschlussbericht.* Freising: Pöyry Forest Industry Consulting GmbH, 2008. 2. 4 Gothe, Dorle, and Ulf Hahne. 18. 5 *The World's Leading Forest Cluster 2030. Forest Cluster Research Strategy.* Helsinki: Finnish Forest Industries, 2013. 6 Gothe, Dorle, and Ulf Hahne. 19.

1 Mixed wood boreal forest in Canada 2 Round-wood 3 Heavily loaded logging truck hauling old growth western red cedar in Canada
4 CLT production 5 Glulam timber production

4

5

Future Developments

Over the last forty years, wood has experienced an unrivaled and dynamic transformation that is unlike that of any other building material. It has been broken down into boards, veneers, strands, and fibers, which have subsequently been reconfigured and reassembled into all kinds of products, most notably large-format beams and panels. While retaining many of its original qualities, the homogenization and optimization of wood's characteristics have turned it into a relevant, versatile, and powerful commodity. The considerable advances made in the development of wood-based composite materials have allowed the emergence of novel construction techniques. In particular, the versatility of solid timber construction has opened up new applications and markets, ensuring that the worldwide demand for wood products will continue to rise. Even though new forest growth currently exceeds annual harvest rates, the long-term supply of sustainably sourced timber will need to be carefully monitored going forward. This is especially important in the light of the growing popularity of wood biomass as a renewable fuel source, which is exerting additional pressure on forest stands.

Wood possesses lower embodied energy levels and causes fewer carbon emissions than other building materials – facts that contribute to its favorable performance when subjected to comprehensive life-cycle assessments. This unique advantage is expected to result in the increased use of timber for mid-rise and high-rise construction, requiring national and local building codes to catch up with what advancements in technology have already made possible. Efforts to impart certain properties or to improve the structural and environmental performance of wood will therefore intensify. Enhanced product manufacturing practices will increase the yield from raw material, ensuring the more efficient use of resources. While it is mostly softwoods that are used for construction, the significant potential of hardwoods for structural applications has been recognized in recent years, leading to innovative product research that is ongoing. Continued concern about the impact of chemicals on human health and the environment are anticipated to give an impetus to research into bio-based adhesives and coatings. Wood-based nanotechnology will allow the development of lightweight, high-strength, composite components with lower energy requirements and smaller environmental footprints than glass fibers, carbon fibers, and polymers derived from oil.[1] New connection technologies such as friction welding will offer non-hazardous alternatives to glues for joining individual wood laminations. Improved techniques for hybrid construction that can easily be disassembled at the end of their service life are projected to address issues of reuse and recycling, while comprehensive open building systems will allow mass customization, satisfying the need for flexibility, economy, and quality control.

The reconfiguration of wood into high-performance products has recently been supplemented by digital fabrication techniques that facilitate the manufacture of almost any shape or form. While virtually anything is possible and the capability for unrestricted experimentation is essential, the use of timber should not be an end in itself. Wood has many advantages over other building materials and numerous technological advances have expanded its use in a variety of applications, but it should be employed in applications that are best in keeping with its unique properties and strengths. Rather than emulating the forms of brick, steel, or concrete construction, contemporary solid timber construction needs to question conventional structural methodologies in order to develop its own tectonic language, with the potential of acquiring a new typology in its own right. While it does not offer an answer to every problem, wood can be employed sensibly alongside other building materials for the creation of safe, healthy, and more sustainable living and working environments, leading to the renewal and revitalization of cities around the world.

1 Rains, Michael T., Alan W. Rudie, and Theodore H. Wegner. "The Promise of Wood-Based Nanotechnology." *The Consultant: Annual Journal of the Association of Consulting Foresters* (2013). 34–39.

1

2

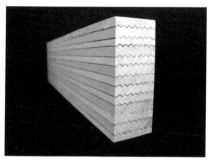

3

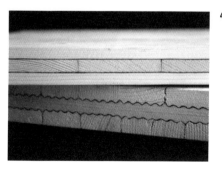

4

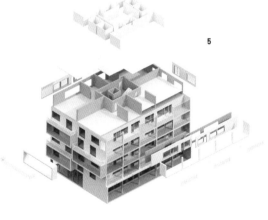

5

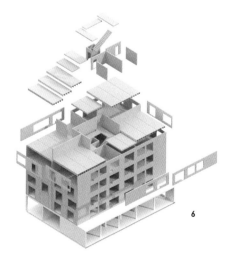

6

7

8

1 Wood-based composite products   **2** The use of hard-woods for structural applications will increase: hybrid glulam beams with top and bottom chords made out of beech   **3** Friction welded glued-laminated timber   **4** Friction welded cross-laminated timber   **5 + 6** Open building system for residential multi-story structures. Concept: Stora Enso.   **7 + 8** Solid timber construction

Biography

Ulrich Dangel is an associate professor and graduate adviser at The University of Texas at Austin, where he teaches graduate and undergraduate courses in design, construction, architectural detailing, and structural design. He received a Diploma in Architecture from Universität Stuttgart in Germany and a Master of Architecture from the University of Oregon. His professional career led him to London where he worked for internationally renowned architectural practices Foster + Partners as well as Grimshaw. He is a registered architect in Germany, the United Kingdom, and Texas and maintains an Austin-based design practice. Ulrich Dangel's research and teaching focus on the use of wood in construction, its influence on building culture and craft, and how it contributes to the advancement of sustainable practices at the scale of local and global economies. Birkhäuser Basel published his first book *Sustainable Architecture in Vorarlberg – Energy Concepts and Construction Systems* in 2010.

Acknowledgments

I would like to acknowledge a number of people who have assisted with the preparation of this book. Several firms, photographers, and organizations generously furnished images without charge, and I am very thankful for their contributions. Kathryn Fernholz, executive director of the nonprofit corporation Dovetail Partners, patiently answered all my questions related to forestry, and I am also extremely grateful for the wealth of environmental information provided by her company's reports. I would particularly like to thank acquisitions editor Alexander Felix and project editor Katharina Kulke at Birkhäuser Basel for their initial review, oversight, and continued advice. My student and research assistant Alena Savera carefully prepared the diagrams and drawings for this book. Her dedicated work is greatly appreciated.

I would like to offer my gratitude to The University of Texas at Austin for its considerable financial support. A faculty research assignment awarded by the Graduate School for the fall semester of 2015 gave me the time necessary to initiate the project, and I also received a subvention grant from the Office of the Vice President for Research. A sincere thank you goes to Dr. Frederick Steiner, former dean of the School of Architecture, who provided me with research assistance. Additionally, a generous publishing grant was provided by Furthermore: a program of the J.M. Kaplan Fund, which helped to cover associated publication expenses.

I am also particularly grateful to my parents, Edith and Gunter Dangel, for their continued advice and encouragement. Finally, this publication could not have happened without the incredible contribution, support, and patience of my wife, Tamie Glass. This book is dedicated to her.

Selected Bibliography

Books

Allen, Edward, and Joseph Iano. *Fundamentals of Building Construction: Materials and Methods.* Hoboken, NJ: J. Wiley & Sons, 2004.

Bernheimer, Andrew, ed. *Timber in the City: Design and Construction in Mass Timber.* New York: ORO Editions, 2014.

Bowyer, Jim L., Rubin Shmulsky, and John G. Haygreen. *Forest Products and Wood Science: An Introduction.* 5th ed. Ames, IA: Blackwell, 2007.

Cheret, Peter, Kurt Schwaner, and Arnim Seidel, eds. *Handbuch und Planungshilfe Urbaner Holzbau: Chancen und Potentiale für die Stadt.* Berlin: DOM Publishers, 2013.

Dangel, Ulrich. *Sustainable Architecture in Vorarlberg: Energy Concepts and Construction Systems.* Basel: Birkhäuser Verlag, 2010.

Deplazes, Andrea. *Constructing Architecture: Materials, Processes, Structures.* Basel: Birkhäuser Verlag, 2005.

Grober, Ulrich. *Die Entdeckung der Nachhaltigkeit: Kulturgeschichte eines Begriffs.* Munich: Verlag Antje Kunstmann, 2013.

Herzog, Thomas, Julius Natterer, Roland Schweitzer, Michael Volz, and Wolfgang Winter. *Timber Construction Manual.* Basel: Birkhäuser Verlag, 2004.

Karacabeyli, Erol, and Brad Douglas, eds. *CLT Handbook: Cross-Laminated Timber.* Pointe-Claire, QC: FPInnovations, Binational Softwood Lumber Council, 2013.

Kaufmann, Hermann, and Winfried Nerdinger, eds. *Building with Timber: Paths into the Future.* Munich: Prestel, 2011.

Kolb, Josef. *Systems in Timber Engineering.* Basel: Birkhäuser Verlag, 2008.

Mayo, Joseph. *Solid Wood: Case Studies in Mass Timber Architecture, Technology and Design.* New York: Routledge, 2015.

Rinke, Mario, and Joseph Schwartz, eds. *Holz: Stoff oder Form.* Sulgen: Niggli, 2014.

Sagmeister, Rudolf, and Kathleen Sagmeister. *Holzbaukunst in Vorarlberg.* Bregenz: Eugen-Ruß-Verlag, 1988.

Schober, Klaus Peter, et al. *Fassaden aus Holz.* Vienna: proHolz Austria, 2010.

Sennett, Richard. *The Craftsman.* New Haven: Yale University Press, 2008.

Steurer, Anton. *Developments in Timber Engineering: The Swiss Contribution.* Basel: Birkhäuser Verlag, 2006.

Wood Handbook: Wood as an Engineering Material. Madison, WI: United States Department of Agriculture, Forest Service, Forest Products Laboratory, 2010.

Reports

Bauen mit Holz = Aktiver Klimaschutz. Munich: Holzforschung München, Technische Universität München, 2010.

Bowyer, Jim, Steve Bratkovich, Alison Lindburg, and Kathryn Fernholz. *Wood Products and Carbon Protocols: Carbon Storage and Low Energy Intensity Should Be Considered.* Minneapolis, MN: Dovetail Partners, 2008.

Bowyer, Jim, Steve Bratkovich, and Kathryn Fernholz. *Utilization of Harvested Wood by the North American Forest Products Industry.* Minneapolis, MN: Dovetail Partners, 2012.

Bowyer, Jim, Steve Bratkovich, Matt Frank, Jeff Howe, Sarah Stai, and Kathryn Fernholz. *Carbon 101: Understanding the Carbon Cycle and the Forest Carbon Debate.* Minneapolis: Dovetail Partners, 2012.

Bowyer, Jim, Steve Bratkovich, Matt Frank, Kathryn Fernholz, Jeff Howe, and Sarah Stai. *Managing Forests for Carbon Mitigation.* Minneapolis: Dovetail Partners, 2011.

Core Writing Team, Rajendra K. Pachauri, and Leo Meyer, eds. *Climate Change 2014: Synthesis Report. Contribution of Working Groups I, II and III to the Fifth Assessment Report of the Intergovernmental Panel on Climate Change.* Geneva: IPCC, 2015.

Cossalter, Christian, and Charlie Pye-Smith. *Fast-Wood Forestry: Myths and Realities.* Bogor: Center for International Forestry Research, 2003.

Crespell, Pablo, and Sylvain Gagnon. *Cross Laminated Timber: A Primer.* Pointe-Claire, QC: FPInnovations, 2010.

Der Wald in Deutschland: Ausgewählte Ergebnisse der dritten Bundeswaldinventur. Berlin: Bundesministerium für Ernährung und Landwirtschaft, 2014.

European Environment Agency. *EEA SIGNALS 2015: Living in a Changing Climate.* Luxembourg: Publications Office of the European Union, 2015

FAO Yearbook of Forest Products 2014. Rome: Food and Agriculture Organization of the United Nations, 2016.

Forest Europe, 2015: State of Europe's Forests 2015. Madrid: Ministerial Conference on the Protection of Forests in Europe, 2015.

Forest Products Annual Market Review 2013–2014. Geneva: United Nations Economic Commission for Europe, Food and Agriculture Organization of the United Nations, 2014.

Global Forest Resources Assessment 2015. Food and Agriculture Organization of the United Nations, 2015.

Green Economy and Trade: Trends, Challenges and Opportunities. Geneva: United Nations Environment Programme, 2013.

HOLZBAUgruppe. *Leader+: Machbarkeitsstudie zum Bauen mit einheimischem Holz im Nordschwarzwald.* Leader+ Aktionsgruppe Nordschwarzwald, 2004.

Holzkonstruktionen in Mischbauweise: Holzbau Handbuch, Reihe 1, Teil 1, Folge 5. Bonn: Holzabsatzfonds, 2006.

mgb ARCHITECTURE + DESIGN, Equilibrium Consulting, LMDG Ltd, and BTY Group. *The Case for Tall Wood Buildings.* Vancouver: 2012.

Salthammer, Tunga, and Rainer Marutzky. *Bauen und Leben mit Holz.* Berlin: Informationsdienst Holz, 2013.

Skidmore, Owings & Merrill, LLP. *Timber Tower Research Project.* Chicago: 2013.

Smith, Ryan E., Gentry Griffin, and Talbot Rice. *Solid Timber Construction: Process, Practice, Performance.* Salt Lake City, UT: University of Utah, Integrated Technology in Architecture Center, College of Architecture and Planning, 2015.

State of the World's Forests 2014. Rome: Food and Agriculture Organization of the United Nations, 2014.

Vital Forest Graphics. United Nations Environment Programme, Food and Agriculture Organization of the United Nations, United Nations Forum on Forests, 2009.

Websites

American Tree Farm System (ATFS)
www.treefarmsystem.org
American Wood Council
www.awc.org
APA – The Engineered Wood Association
www.apawood.org
Binational Softwood Lumber Council (BSLC)
www.softwoodlumber.org
Canadian Sustainable Forest Management
www.csasfmforests.ca
Canadian Wood Council
www.cwc.ca
Center for International Forestry Research (CIFOR)
www.cifor.org
Dovetail Partners
www.dovetailinc.org
Food and Agriculture Organization of the United Nations – Forestry
www.fao.org/forestry
Forestry Innovation Investment (FII)
www.bcfii.ca
Forest Stewardship Council (FSC)
www.fsc.org
forum holzbau
www.forum-holzbau.com
FPInnovations
www.fpinnovations.ca

Holzforschung Austria
www.holzforschung.at
Informationsdienst Holz
www.informationsdienst-holz.de
Lignum – Holzwirtschaft Schweiz
www.lignum.ch
NASA Global Climate Change – Vital Signs of the Planet
climate.nasa.gov
naturally:wood
www.naturallywood.com
Programme for the Endorsement of Forest Certification (PEFC)
www.pefc.org
pro:Holz Austria
www.proholz.at
ReThink Wood
www.rethinkwood.com
Sustainable Forestry Initiative (SFC)
www.sfiprogram.org
USDA Forest Products Laboratory
www.fpl.fs.fed.us
Wood for Good
www.woodforgood.com
WoodWorks – Wood Products Council
www.woodworks.org

Illustration Credits

American Tree Farm System (ATFS): p. 39 / fig. 7
American Wood Council: p. 67 / fig. 6, 8+9
APA – The Engineered Wood Association: p. 47 / fig. 4; p. 105 / fig. 1–4
Auroralight (www.dreamstime.com): p. 180 / fig. 3
Bauer Holzbausysteme: p. 177 / fig. 4+5
BB&S Treated Lumber of New England: p. 145 / fig. 15
Stéphane Bidouze (www.dreamstime.com): p. 15 / fig. 4; p. 79 / fig. 1
www.binderholz.com: p. 95 / fig. 17; p. 159 / fig. 11
Blumer-Lehmann AG: p. 83 / fig. 10, 13+14; p. 95 / fig. 18; p. 124 / fig. 9; p. 125 / fig. 10–12; p. 130 / fig. 2; p. 159 / fig. 9
Friedrich Böhringer: p. 81 / fig. 5; p. 91 / fig. 4
Boise Cascade: p. 118 / fig. 4; p. 184 / fig. 1
Bernd Borchardt: p. 163 / fig. 2
Jolene Byford, Ashley Harris: p. 94 / fig. 12
Canadian Standards Association Group – Sustainable Forest Management System: p. 39 / fig. 6
Boonsom Chotpaiboonpun (www.depositphotos.com): p. 48 / fig. 7
Rob Cicchetti (www.depositphotos.com): p. 90 / fig. 2
Ulrich Dangel: p. 38 / fig. 1; p. 91 / fig. 3+5; p. 111 / fig. 1; p. 134 / fig. 2–4; p. 142 / fig. 2+4; p. 143 / fig. 5–8; p. 144 / fig. 9; p. 145 / fig. 12–14; p. 150 / fig. 2; p. 180 / fig. 2
Dainis Derics (www.depositphotos.com): p. 142 / fig. 3
EPFL Lausanne, IBOIS, Laboratory for Timber Construction: p. 184 / fig. 3+4
Equilibrium Consulting: p. 113 / fig. 8

Erne AG Holzbau: p. 124 / fig. 8

ETH Zurich, Institute of Structural Engineering (IBK):
p. 112 / fig. 5

Fagus Jura SA: p. 184 / fig. 2

Johannes Fink (courtesy of Kaufmann Bausysteme):
p. 83 / fig. 11; p. 118 / fig. 6; p. 130 / fig. 3;
p. 176 / fig. 1

Forest Products Association of Canada (courtesy of
Forestry Innovation Investment): p. 35 / fig. 10;
p. 71 / fig. 2

Forest Stewardship Council (FSC): p. 39 / fig. 3

FPInnovations: p. 170 / fig. 3–5

Leszek Glasner (www.depositphotos.com):
p. 145 / fig. 11

Michael Green Architecture: p. 172 / fig. 11

Stéphane Groleau (courtesy of Nordic Structures): p. 66
/ fig. 4+5; p. 111 / fig. 2+3; p. 151 / fig. 3–4

Gumpp & Maier GmbH: p. 177 / fig. 6+7

Hartl Haus: p. 94 / fig. 13–15

Huber & Sohn: p. 118 / fig. 5; p. 131 / fig. 4; p. 171 /
fig. 8+9

Hans Hundegger AG: p. 123 / fig. 3–5; p. 124 / fig. 6+7

Dr. Richard Huter, Bregenz: p. 117 / fig. 1

Matthias Kabel: p. 60 / fig. 3

KAMPA GmbH: p. 171 / fig. 7

Tatiana Karaseva (www.depositphotos.com):
p. 81 / fig. 3

Architekten Hermann Kaufmann ZT GmbH:
cover photo; p. 61 / fig. 4+5; p. 82 / fig. 6+7;
p. 113 / fig. 9; p. 119 / fig. 9

Electra Kay-Smith (www.depositphotos.com):
p. 71 / fig. 3

Martin Lukas Kim: p. 164 / fig. 4

KLH Massivholz GmbH: p. 97 / fig. 22

KLH UK: p. 53 / fig. 5; p. 67 / fig. 7; p. 96 / fig. 20;
p. 97 / fig. 21; p. 112 / fig. 6; p. 159 / fig. 10

Emily Knapp: p. 93 / fig. 9+10

Dmitri Kotchetov (www.depositphotos.com):
p. 134 / fig. 1

Lev Kropotov (www.depositphotos.com): p. 93 / fig. 11

lattkearchitekten, Augsburg: p. 164 / fig. 5+6

Ilona Legenkaja (www.depositphotos.com): p. 80 / fig. 2

Lerka555 (www.dreamstime.com): p. 14 / fig. 3

Lichtblau Architekten: p. 165 / fig. 7–9

Olaf Mahlstedt: p. 176 / fig. 2+3

Master Sgt. Jeremy Lock (U.S. Air Force): p. 26–27 / fig. 1

Michael Meuter, Zurich (LIGNUM): p. 46 / fig. 1; p. 47 /
fig. 3; p. 48 / fig. 5; p. 53 / fig. 3; p. 92 / fig. 7

Microtec: p. 57 / fig. 5–7

Claire Miller, Layla Salameh, Alena Savera: p. 95 / fig. 16

www.mm-holz.com: p. 82 / fig. 8; p. 107 / fig. 11+13;
p. 118 / fig. 3; p. 130 / fig. 1; p. 131 / fig. 5

MMK Holz-Beton-Fertigteile GmbH: p. 113 / fig. 7+10

Roland Nagy (www.depositphotos.com): p. 157 / fig. 1

NASA Earth Observatory: p. 18 / fig. 2; p. 23 / fig. 4+6

NASA Johnson Space Center, Earth Science and
Remote Sensing Unit (eol.jsc.nasa.gov):
p. 18 / fig. 3

National Snow and Ice Data Center: p. 23 / fig. 5
(1941 photo courtesy of Ulysses William O. Field;
2004 photo courtesy of Bruce F. Molnia)

www.naturallywood.com (courtesy of Forestry
Innovation Investment): p. 28 / fig. 2; p. 29 /
fig. 5+6; p. 33 / fig. 2+3; p. 34 / fig. 4-6; p. 35 /
fig. 8+9; p. 56 / fig. 2+3; p. 180 / fig. 1

Elena Odareeva (www.depositphotos.com): p. 157 / fig. 3

Nikolai Okhitin (www.depositphotos.com): p. 135 / fig. 5

Leung Cho Pan (www.depositphotos.com): p. 157 / fig. 2

Ema Peter (courtesy of Equilibrium Consulting):
p. 150 / fig. 1; p. 171 / fig. 10

Nichaya Praditsup (www.depositphotos.com):
p. 49 / fig. 8

Programme for the Endorsement of Forest Certification
(PEFC): p. 39 / fig. 4

Will Pryce (courtesy of Waugh Thistleton Architects):
p. 158 / fig. 4–6; p. 185 / fig. 8

Norman Radon (courtesy of Kaufmann Bausysteme):
p. 83 / fig. 12

Reclaimed Space: p. 61 / fig. 6

Dominik Reipka: p. 164 / fig. 3

Hubert Rieß: p. 119 / fig. 8

Vitaly Romanovich (www.depositphotos.com):
p. 140–141 / fig. 1

Federico Rostagno (www.depositphotos.com):
p. 49 / fig. 10

Tacio Philip Sansonovski (www.depositphotos.com):
p. 72–73 / fig. 4

Alena Savera: p. 14 / fig. 1 (based on data from:
www.grida.no); p. 14 / fig. 2; p. 18 / fig. 1
(based on data from: Global Forest Resources
Assessment 2015, The Food and Agriculture
Organization of the United Nations); p. 22 / fig. 1
(based on data from: climate.nasa.gov: Vostok ice
core data/J.R. Petit et al.; NOAA Mauna Loa CO_2
record.); p. 22 / fig. 2 (based on data from: climate.
nasa.gov: NASA's Goddard Institute for Space
Studies); p. 22 / fig. 3; p. 28 / fig. 3; p. 38 /
fig. 2 (based on data from: FSC Facts & Figures,
Dec. 1, 2015 and PEFC Global Statistics, Nov.
2015); p. 52 / fig. 1 (based on: *Bauen mit Holz =
Aktiver Klimaschutz*. Munich: Holzforschung
München, Technische Universität München,
2010); p. 52 / fig. 2 (based on data from: Bowyer,
Jim, Steve Bratkovich, Alison Lindburg, and
Kathryn Fernholz. *Wood Products and Carbon
Protocols: Carbon Storage and Low Energy
Intensity Should Be Considere*d. Minneapolis, MN:
Dovetail Partners, 2008); p. 56 / fig. 1 (based on
data from: Bowyer, Jim, Steve Bratkovich, and
Kathryn Fernholz. *Utilization of Harvested Wood
by the North American Forest Products Industry*.
Minneapolis, MN: Dovetail Partners, 2012); p. 60 /
fig. 1 (based on: Salthammer, Tunga, and Rainer
Marutzky. *Bauen und Leben mit Holz*. Berlin:
Informationsdienst Holz, 2013); p. 65 / fig. 1;
p. 90 / fig. 1; p. 92 / fig. 6; p. 96 / fig. 19; p. 117 /
fig. 2 (based on: "Die Logik der Vorfertigung:

Eine Systemübersicht". *Zeitschrift über Holz als Werkstoff und Werke in Holz* 13.50 (2013). 12–13. p. 144 / fig. 10; p. 163 / fig. 1; p. 170 / fig. 2
Jakob Schärer: p. 170 / fig. 1
Schankula Architekten: p. 171 / fig. 6
Hans-Peter Schiess: p. 135 / fig. 6
www.schreinerkastler.at (courtesy of Milestones in Communication): p. 172 / fig. 12
Eleni Seitanidou (www.depositphotos.com): p. 81 / fig. 4
Daniel Shearling, Ramboll (courtesy of Waugh Thistleton Architects): p. 158 / fig. 7; p. 159 / fig. 8
Skidmore, Owings & Merrill: p. 172 / fig. 13; p. 173 / fig. 14
Tobias Smith: p. 112 / fig. 4
Tom Spilliaert (www.depositphotos.com): p. 60 / fig. 2
Stora Enso: p. 47 / fig. 2; p. 48 / fig. 6; p. 53 / fig. 4; p. 106 / fig. 7; p. 107 / fig. 14; p. 118 / fig. 7; p. 181 / fig. 4; p. 184 / fig. 5+6; p. 185 / fig. 7
StructureCraft: p. 106 / fig. 8
Structurlam: p. 65 / fig. 3
Sustainable Forestry Initiative (SFI): p. 39 / fig. 5
Taikoko Shoin Co. Ltd. (courtesy of Forestry Innovation Investment): p. 57 / fig. 4
Martin Tessler (courtesy of Equilibrium Consulting): p. 65 / fig. 2
ThomaHolz: p. 106 / fig. 9+10
Neil P. Thompson: p. 35 / fig. 7
Nicholas A. Tonelli: p. 15 / fig. 5
Vorarlberger Landesbibliothek, Vorarlberg-Sammlungen, Helmut Klapper: p. 123 / fig. 1
Weyerhaeuser: p. 105 / fig. 5+6
WIEHAG GmbH – Timber Construction: p. 82 / fig. 9; p. 107 / fig. 12; p. 151 / fig. 5; p. 181 / fig. 5
Dave Willman (www.depositphotos.com): p. 123 / fig. 2
Alexey Yagovkin (www.depositphotos.com): p. 71 / fig. 1
Tewan Yangmee (www.depositphotos.com): p. 49 / fig. 9

From other publications:
Hannß Carl von Carlowitz, 1713: *Sylvicultura Oeconomica, oder Haußwirthliche Nachricht und Naturmäßige Anweisung zur Wilden Baum-Zucht:* p. 33 / fig. 1
United Nations Environment Programme (UNEP), 2010: *The Latin America and the Caribbean Atlas of our Changing Environment:* p. 19 / fig. 5+6

Imprint

Copy editing Richard Toovey
Project management Alexander Felix, Katharina Kulke
Production Heike Strempel
Layout, cover design and typesetting Jenna Gesse
Paper Magno natural, 120 g/m²
Printing Beltz Bad Langensalza GmbH

Library of Congress Cataloging-in-Publication data
A CIP catalog record for this book has been applied for at the Library of Congress.

Bibliographic information published by the German National Library: The German National Library lists this publication in the Deutsche Nationalbibliografie; detailed bibliographic data are available on the Internet at http://dnb.dnb.de.

This publication is also available as an e-book (ISBN PDF 978-3-0356-0863-2; ISBN EPUB 978-3-0356-0851-9) and in a German language edition (ISBN 978-3-0356-1027-7).

© 2017 Birkhäuser Verlag GmbH, Basel
P.O. Box 44, 4009 Basel, Switzerland
Part of Walter de Gruyter GmbH, Berlin/Boston

Printed on acid-free paper produced from chlorine-free pulp. TCF ∞

With the generous support of
Furthermore: a program of the J.M. Kaplan Fund

Printed in Germany

ISBN 978-3-0356-1025-3

9 8 7 6 5 4 3 2 1   www.birkhauser.com